Here's Jonny:

Tales of Gratitude from the Oilfield to the Boardroom

By Jonny Fowler

Here's Jonny:

Tales of Gratitude from the Oilfield to the Boardroom

ISBN: 9781792795954

Imprint: Independently published

Cover design by Sooraj Mathew

Edited by Hilary Jastram

Dedication

To my dad, my treasured wife, Cassy (my Carmela Soprano) and the rest of my family, the co-conspirators in my life who I love beyond description. Without you, my existence means nothing.

Resources

Facebook:

https://www.facebook.com/jonnyfowler68

Celebrity Facebook:

https://www.facebook.com/HeresJonnyFowler/

Instagram:

@heresjonnyfowler

LinkedIn:

https://www.linkedin.com/in/jonnyfowler/

Table of Contents

Preface

I remember it like it was yesterday...

Jonny Fowler walked into the room of the 5th story Aqualounge of the high rise I lived in. We'd made special arrangements for him to spend two days with me there working out a business plan.

After the two days were over, he stood up, thanked me and said: "Okay, off to work!"

The moment I shook his hand, I knew Jonny was a guy who does not f*ck around. Even though he's a banker, he has a rugged exterior that only someone who has seen significant shit possesses.

A few weeks later, Jonny paid and showed up for two more days. He brought along a guy he had hired, and he wanted me to teach the guy to do the work from my trainings.

At the same time, Jonny was running with the playbook and hiring software engineers from overseas to build a system that would automate the entire process I'd taught him.

That was in 2015, and Jonny has been working side by side with me since. He's attended more of my events than any other person in my network.

Because of that, I've gotten to know him well.

I was right. He has seen a lot. He came from real humble beginnings and has worked his way up to the one percent.

As a matter of fact, Jonny has not only lived through tragedy and hardship in his personal life; he's dealt with massive stress in corporate situations as well. From running one of the largest mortgage companies in America to having to sue that same company just to get paid what was owed to him, but despite all of the setbacks in his life, he's void of excuses.

He does the work and has reaped the rewards accordingly. Currently, Jonny runs a nationwide mortgage company that produces multi-nine figures of mortgage-backed securities per year.

His company is the single largest real estate advertiser on Facebook. They've created thousands of sales funnels.

This book is Jonny's story, and the lessons in this book are worth a fortune to those wise enough to learn them.

Lastly, if you're in the mortgage industry and you want to team up with the most innovative leader I know, Jonny is your guy.

~Ryan Stewman
CEO, Break Free Academy

Introduction

My story is not unfamiliar, but it is mine. I came from humble beginnings, and when I think of my story, I envision the buildings where my life began, where my career grew and where I live now. The reason I am sharing it with you is to bring value to you in your life and career.

Whether you are looking to make a change in careers or excel in the one you have now, there is a section in this book for you!!

Read on for lessons in learning your own value and the value of your business (pages 66 and 115) and understanding the importance of maintaining integrity in your career (page 100). Discover valuable advice for creating your own business (beginning on page 99), marketing (page 102) and education and training (page 143)—all of which play a role in being a successful employer!

Failure can sometimes be the greatest path to success!

Whatever your goal in reading *Here's Jonny: Tales of Gratitude from the Oilfield to the Boardroom*, I guarantee there is a section of this book that will call to you and give you the tools you need to be a greater version of yourself.

Enjoy!!

Foreword

I remember telling Jonny before we embarked on our first trip together: "If you have things to do I can just go alone." I said this to let him off the hook. I said this because we had just met in person a couple of days prior. I said this because Jonny had agreed, seemingly whimsically. I said this because Jonny was surrounded by what I saw as endless professional opportunities.

We were in Nashville, Tennessee and I needed to get to Houston, Texas. My chosen means of transportation was to drive the nearly thousand miles. I wanted to take the opportunity to see parts of Mississippi, Louisiana, and Alabama that I probably never would have the chance to see again. I wanted to do the grueling drive through what Jonny had probably seen a thousand times. After all, this was the area that surrounded where Jonny grew up as a child.

When Jonny said he'd drop his flight and take this drive with me, I was surprised. To my mind, he didn't appear to have put any thought into the decision. He simply said yes to a pretty big commitment of a rather dull drive at the expense of opportunity and comfort. Nevertheless, 45 minutes later we were in the car and off on our 3-day excursion across the South.

One thing I learned very clearly on that trip; is that when Jonny says "yes" to a commitment, he means it. It doesn't matter how large or how small; it doesn't matter with whom; Jonny is a rare throwback. You don't need to watch his deeds to believe his words because Jonny's word *is* his bond. When he says he is going to do something, big or small, he *always* follows through. This became very apparent to me when I offered Jonny an out on our trip, and that wasn't an option for him because he had said yes.

If you've ever spent three days in a car with a relative stranger, you learn quite a bit about the person sitting shotgun.

Having been in the mortgage business for over two decades, I have the ability to gauge the nature of most salespeople.

We are a breed that likes to talk about our personal success, accurate or not. Salespeople always catch the biggest fish, especially when there's no witness. However, that wasn't the case on our little drive across the South.

We bounced along the Mississippi and drove the 18-plus miles of the Atchafalaya Basin Bridge. Jonny's default conversation always came back to his team: his loan officers. Jonny didn't use this time to boast of his sole success. That's usually what people do when given the rare chance to set the narrative about themselves with a shiny new friend. No, Jonny talked about the loan officers he recruited, who he works with.

"You ought to see what Chad's doing" or "Jenni's a star and tough as nails." To use only a couple of examples is a disservice to his team, but if I were to tell you all the stories and details about his team he shared on that drive, I'd be the one writing the book, not the foreword.

Let me just tell you, his share of the conversation was all about his team, regardless of production or other variations. I think that says it best.

Jonny Fowler is a throwback; a hard-working, tough as nails man who could boast but chooses humility. He is someone who will outwork you and only speak of other's efforts. He is that rarest of breed whose word is his bond on matters both easy (and as I learned) hard. In the coming pages, you will embark on your own little journey with Jonny. I imagine you will learn the same qualities I learned on my trip. Most of all I think you'll learn or at least be inspired, through some of his life stories, to reflect and become a better version of yourself. As he said, he wants that for you.

We are all on journeys of some sort, and we can always use a little shine along our roads. Jonny has gifted me with some of his shine, and for that, I call him my dear friend.

~Brian Stevens
Founder, MortgageShots; National Real Estate Post
Owner, Listing Booster; PreApp 1003

Section I

Just a Good Ol' Boy

Chapter 1: Texas Born

"You may all go to hell, and I will go to Texas."

~Davy Crockett

I told myself, If I ever make $250K in a year, I am buying myself a Rolex. I did it, and it wasn't even that hard.

But I sure as hell had a rough start.

When I was born on August 12, 1968, in Texarkana, Texas, my father was in college and had two jobs. My mother was a stay-at-home mom. My dad had just turned 20, and my mom was going to be 19 years old. We were a very young family living in a two-bedroom single-wide trailer.

My father was born in Hope, Arkansas and went to school with Bill Clinton until Bill moved away. One of the funniest things that I remember about Bill Clinton is my grandmother who lived in Hope, Arkansas, telling me that, "You're damn right, I voted for Bill Clinton for president. I would do anything to get him the f*ck out of Arkansas."

My mother was a high school beauty queen and was absolutely beautiful. She was a fraternal twin to a brother and how those two match-up is still funny to me because she's a little, bitty, tiny, blond woman and he's a great big, burly, dark guy. She was born in New Orleans and grew up in New Iberia, Louisiana. She was a wonderful, caring woman who wanted to make sure that my brother and I had everything that we needed, that we were loved, and that we were cared for. I remember going Christmas shopping when we were old enough to know who Santa Claus was, and she wanted to buy my brother, and I bicycles for Christmas. When the salespeople said they would not be ready in time for Christmas, my mother threatened the guy to make sure that whatever they had to do on those bikes was finished on that night because we were taking them. And by God, we loaded up those bicycles in the back of my mother's car and took them home that evening because her kids were not going to go without bicycles for Christmas.

She liked traveling when she was younger, and to this day still spends her free time with us. She is a loving, thoughtful, highly intelligent woman. At almost 70 years old, she remains stunning.

When I was two years old, my dad became a maintenance engineer at a company in the food industry right outside of Houston, Texas. So, we loaded up our trailer and moved down to Alvin, Texas. We lived in Alvin for quite some time, then moved to Manvel, Texas. In 1972, my mother was pregnant again and having complications.

One of my first memories is my parents shipping me off somewhere during the time she was pregnant. I don't remember where I wound up, but I stayed with someone in the family for a while. When I came home, my parents had to explain to me that we had lost my little brother, Jeremy.

At the time this happened, of course, I couldn't appreciate or understand how poor we were. Kids don't realize how poor they are. So as the years went by, all I am told is that we were so poor that the cemetery had to donate the grave site to us.

People took up a collection at my parent's church to pay for the headstone, and my father had to actually dig the grave to bury my little brother. My middle brother is still in the same spot where he was buried in Manvel, Texas. My wife,

Cassy, and I go by and see the headstone every once in a while.

In the spring and summer of 1974, life would take another turn when I would learn about the concept of Christmas in July.

I've always felt that Christmas in July was meant for me. After my mother's pregnancy and Jeremy passing away, my mother was pregnant again.

My parents were worried about having complications with this pregnancy like they'd had with the previous one, so once again, they sent me to my aunt's house (where I still can't remember going the first time).

When everything was all clear, my aunt brought me back home to our house, and on July 1, 1974, my little brother was born. That's why I think they call it Christmas in July, because that July, I got the greatest gift I could ever get, a little brother to take care of and call my very own. I was ecstatic when Cory Lane Fowler was born.

We have been as thick as thieves throughout the years. I started babysitting him and taking care of him when he was three, and I was nine. We would run all over the streets of Spring Branch, which was a suburb of Houston, Texas.

Throughout the years, we have become the best of friends and remain that way. We've worked together a few times. But even though he is grown up, he is still my little brother and I always, always, always make sure that he's taken care of. I was his best man at his wedding. He is somebody who is near and dear and closer to me than anybody else in this world.

Shortly after my brother died, we moved to Houston, Texas and for the first time in my life, I felt somewhat normal. Our house was on a slab foundation, and it was a cool feeling to be in a real house and not a trailer for once. I started first grade and my brother, and I had our own rooms.

I was a hyperactive child. Back then, they didn't have the label or diagnosis of ADD. But all I know was that I was a hyper kid and not good at sitting still. I found school very boring. As a matter of fact, in third grade, the school called my father to visit, so he could sit in the coat room to observe me. Well, I would get tired of my desk being where it was, so I would get up and move my desk over by the window. That way I could see better. I would walk out of class and go across the street to the Stop-N-Go and play video games or buy *Star Wars* cards or whatever else I wanted to do.

I guess I've never sat still very well. I always have to be stimulated and need something to do.

When I was in my teens, I realized what money was. At that time, we lived out in the country, and I would throw hay, clean horse stalls, and do whatever chores I could for money. I really enjoyed it. We lived in the middle of f*cking nowhere. It took forever to go anywhere, and my dad had moved us out there because he thought it would be safer than living in Houston.

One of the first memories I have about moving out to the country is that every grade rode the same school bus. Meaning all the kids from kindergarten to the seniors in high school were on the same school bus. The bus would stop and let you out in the student smoking area, and the first day I got off the bus at school and walked through the student smoking area. I thought that was hilarious. *I'm strolling right past these guys with a snuff can in their back pocket and a f*cking knife on their side.* I thought *yeah, this is a whole lot safer than Houston.*

That wasn't the first move I made. I went to three different elementary schools, five different junior highs, and three high schools. Even though we remained in the same area, for some reason, we moved a lot.

Despite steering clear of the kids hanging out and smoking and all the moving we did, I made good friends when I was young. I have always valued true, real friendships like the ones I found with Reid Cashdollar, Scott Hogan, Chris Merino, Gerry Toloudis. These are people who are still important to me. My elementary school girlfriend was Kim Craft, and her sister was Pammy. I am still friends with both of them and their mother.

My friends became my family, and it has been this way my whole life. I've always been surrounded by people who I love, care for and trust. Any of my high school friends will tell you that we had a family. Any of my coworkers that I work with at Hancock Mortgage Partners will tell you that we are a family.

We ended up moving back to Spring Branch in Houston Texas, and I got thrown out of high school in my junior year after being told I was too disruptive and independent to fit into the public education system. When I look back on that moment, it's funny to me. Having wound up where I am now, I get a kick out of it.

I was never a fan of school. Now, as I am writing this book, the week before I turn 50, I think our school system is a joke. At least it is for people like me. School didn't teach me all that much that I couldn't have learned in one year, on my own. My teachers taught me how to roll a condom onto a banana, but they never told me how to write a resume. They didn't tell me how to interview for a job. They didn't tell me what a job was, or what working in a job meant. They didn't tell me anything that had to deal with real life.

School never told me a f*cking thing about taxes, or building permits, or what the real world needs you to know. But by God, I remember how to put a condom on a banana. Way to go health class.

School rips off our kids today. Public school, especially, is a damn shame. I remember spending hours, days and weeks, studying for stupid standardized tests. I didn't find out why I was studying what I was, until later in life, when I discovered it's because the schools get subsidization for the people who pass. You're supposed to be learning and getting an education, but the system has turned into a business for funding. It's a horrible joke.

When I was escorted out of school at 18, I hadn't graduated, and the year was 1986.

We had just moved back to Houston from a little town called Waller, Texas, and I had one of my first real jobs at a gas station in Memorial, Texas and was even paying taxes.

My boss was a Greek guy, and he taught me a life lesson I have never forgotten.

One day, my boss had lost something—what it was isn't important. As he was frantically looking for whatever it was, he told me to go jump into the dumpster and look for it. I shot him a look like he was absolutely crazy and said, "Not a chance. I'm not going in there." He said, "No, seriously. I need you to get in the dumpster and see if it's in there." I told him again, "I'm not getting in the dumpster."

He walked past me, climbed into the dumpster, spent less than 30 seconds in there, then hopped back up. Whatever he was looking for was in his hand. As he walked toward me, his face was a mixture of anger and frustration. I thought he was either fixing to hit me or scream at me. In this life lesson that I'll remember forever, he stared me dead square in my eye and said, "I will never ask you to do something that I wouldn't do myself." Then, he turned around and walked off.

That memory has stuck with me from that age, and I use this life lesson even now. Anything you ever ask anybody else to do, you better be willing to do yourself. If you're not willing to do it yourself, it may not be the right action to take.

Sarandos Theocharidis (Sandy) and I are still friends, and we go to lunch together every once in a while.

When this life lesson hit, I had two jobs and was going to school. In addition to spending time at the gas station, where I performed tasks like doing oil changes and fixing minor mechanical crap, I delivered pizza. That schedule continued for probably another year or so. Then I began to work part-time for my father.

He worked for an original equipment manufacturer in the oilfield business. Because I could work for him in the chemical plants and oil plants as temporary labor I did that during holidays, and summer vacations. While I was there, I actually thought I was going to be a millionaire because I was making $10 an hour. In total, I worked about 100 hours a week, and so also got paid $15 an hour in overtime.

I figured after about two months of working; I would retire. Of course, I didn't realize one, how addictive money was, and two, that money is cool. I stayed on part-time for a while and did not become a millionaire. When the manufacturer gave me an assignment for a job out of town,

I left the pizza place before my shift was over the night before I was to leave. The deal was you had to wait until everybody else finished their jobs. Well, some people were f*cking lazy and slow, and I wasn't going to wait on them. So, I did what I was supposed to do, and I left. Then...I ended up getting fired.

Shortly after that, I also quit the gas station because I was bored. I thought, again, since I was making $250 a week in salary, *that money is all mine, baby*. When I started making that much money is when I learned about taxes because I didn't know who the f*ck this FICA person was. I remember the first time I got what I thought was a big paycheck—I actually called a buddy of mine whose mom worked in payroll. Both of us couldn't believe how much money they had taken out of my check because $250 a week was a sh*tload of money. But then they took $38 out of my check, and I didn't know who was getting it.

Still in the money-making mode, I started my own business at 19. A buddy and I worked on automotive air conditioning for car dealerships. I had been on my own since I'd moved out at 17 years old.

Since I was on my own and working in a job that was making me good money, I got up to all sorts of adventures. One of my craziest decisions landed me in jail. While on spring break in Galveston, Texas with friends, we stopped on the side of the road. We were all pretty drunk by this time when some guy walked in wearing the funniest outfit I had ever seen. He was a bicycle rider and back in the day people wore helmets that looked like alien heads.

He was wearing a helmet and ridiculous shorts, and I just started laughing. I couldn't help it. It was especially funny because I was wasted. The owner of the store threw me outside, and I told him to f*ck off. He dropped everything he was doing, glared at me and asked me, "You want to fight?"

I guess I did because we walked outside where a cop was waiting for me. That was the first time I learned about public intoxication. He hooked me up, threw me in the back of the cop car and I spent my first couple days ever in jail. When I got out, my dad was out of town, and I was too embarrassed to go home.

That's what led to me moving out the first time, and I didn't go back home for a few years after that.

When I started that little company doing the automotive air conditioning, I thought I wanted to mess with cars for the rest of my life.

But, after a couple of years, I realized it was not what I wanted to do.

Working on cars is a pain in the ass. It's hot; they're dirty; it's sweaty. It wasn't for me.

The job that I was doing for the oilfield manufacturing company was the perfect segue into what I wanted to do next because they had so much business. I was able to work more than full time but could also go three weeks or a month without a job. I was 19 when I made about $63,000, and that was back in 1987. It was my first big-time taste of money.

Since high school hadn't taught me a f*cking thing about money, I spent as much as I brought in. Being on the edge of broke kept me in that job from 19 years of age until I was in my early thirties. I hated almost every day of it.

The politics were insane. The travel was outrageous. In my last year, I traveled to 13 different countries in 12 months. One morning, I woke up and wasn't sure where I was. I had just spent about 100 days in Egypt. Then I'd gotten on a plane to go to Paris for 30-plus days before getting on another plane. After all that travel, when I woke up after getting to my hotel the night before, I turned on the television, and at the time, didn't know there was a different language outside of Spanish. I wanted any kind of clue to help me remember what country I was in. The language coming out of the TV sounded like Spanish, but it wasn't.

Finally, I figured out I was in f*cking Sao Paulo, Brazil. When I couldn't keep track of what country I was in, that was my wakeup call. I knew it was time to quit. I wasn't enjoying what I was doing anymore. I stayed on in Brazil for more than a month. By the time I made the decision to pull the plug, I had traveled so much with the company, for so many years that I don't remember the 90s at all. I completely missed grunge rock because I was working.

In the oilfield, you have to be on the job at six o'clock in the morning. That means I had to get up at four o'clock in the morning. I'm not a morning person. I hate it. Later, as I've paid attention in life, I've realized you don't have to be at work at six o'clock in the morning. Those hours are kept by the people who I call clock-riders--the people who are trying to steal money by working overtime every single day and being busy instead of doing business.

My whole life, since I've gotten out of high school, has been basically on the road. One of the things I appreciate about my travels is that I could learn about different cultures as I was exposed to all kinds of new landscapes and art. I could appreciate unfamiliar traditions. Traveling helps you put into perspective what is important to you and what isn't.

I realized when I traveled that even though I thought we had grown up poor in a two-bedroom single-wide trailer that other people in an impoverished country would not view our lives like that. That definitely helps to shift your viewpoint. If you don't want to be poor, and you live in this country, it is not acceptable that you are poor. In the US, you can do anything you want to get ahead. Anybody can start their own business. Anybody can make something of themselves and come up with a better idea for the marketplace. I don't give a damn who says that you can't do it either because you can. I have seen people do this firsthand, and I know it is far easier to succeed in this country than it is in other countries.

Now, the flip side is that this country tries to suppress you and hold you back. It overregulates you, depending on who's in office, but, it is still quite possible that anybody if they wanted to, could become a millionaire, billionaire, or even make more money than that. I adore this fact about this country, and it keeps me coming back every year.

Back in those days, there was a company called Brown and Root. I didn't work for Brown and Root, but I felt about them the way I felt about my gig in the oil business. Brown and Root's logo was a "B" and an "R," and the joke in the industry was that the "B" and "R" didn't stand for Brown and Root; it stood for brothers-in-law and relatives. The joke was you never knew who you were going to work for the next day.

I was never going to hire one of my friends just because they were my friend. I've always told people, "If my mother worked for me and she wasn't doing a good job, I'd fire her." I don't feel a duty to hire people I know. Just the way that not everyone deserves a house, not everyone deserves a job. If you're not going to do your job, get out of the way; let somebody else do it because it's not my duty to babysit you as an adult, or keep you out of the smoking area.

We're all here to support the people who bring in the revenue. That's what our job is. If you don't like it, go somewhere else. Go screw with someone else because I don't have time for you to screw with me. That's why I was never going to hire someone to work with me just because they were my friend. I wouldn't cross that boundary. I also was not going to hire family members or relatives simply because of our relationships. To be clear, I do have family members and relatives who work with me and vice versa. But they all deserve their jobs. Conversely, I've had some relatives ask me for jobs, and I have denied them for good reasons. I don't want to work with people who aren't hard workers and who play hide-and-seek for $2,000 a week. All they do is create more work for me. And I'm already busy enough.

On one of my jobs, I had a dozen guys working for me. I was reporting to an engineer who had gotten out of college the day before. He told me as I was taking apart a certain piece of equipment to let him see it. Being the mechanic that I am, I asked him, "Is there something I need to know?" He said, "No." So, I said, "Well, is it vibrating? Does it have a high temperature? This is what I need to know when I'm taking it apart." He replied, "No, no, no. I've designed a whole bunch of these things, but I've never seen what one looks like." I thought to myself *I'm working for this guy. He's never seen what it is that I'm taking apart and what I'm fixing to rebuild and put back together. Yet, he's also going take the glory for the job well-done.*

Chapter 2: On the Road Again...and Again...and Again

The world is a book, and those who do not travel read only a page." ~Unknown

I've spent half my life in Mexico, but I've been to Northern Africa, all over Europe, to South and Central America, and have visited every state in this continent, including Alaska and Hawaii. That's why now, for me to travel 40 weeks a year is a joke. Because before, I was all over the freaking world. I've been to some real sh*thole places too. I'm pretty sure I coined that phrase before Trump.

I learned a lot from traveling, and also got my first taste of what we call news or today's media. I know now it's frosting. The news is complete bullsh*t. So, if you're watching the news here in the states, pay attention to what they're telling you and wanting you to learn, or listen to because if you end up in Europe and you're watching the BBC, it's totally different than what you're being fed here. You can get better information about what's going on in the world by watching Al-Jazeera than you ever can by watching ABC, CBS, NBC and especially, CNN.

People here think they're free, but we're so censored we have no clue what reality is. That was just one of the insights that traveling taught me—no matter what they say on television unless you've been there, you don't have a clue about the truth.

Maybe I can handle the truth better than other people because, even though this may sound strange, I don't really have feelings. I might have become a little jaded, or maybe it's due to the fact I grew up in the South, and my feelings have to do with what I was taught. Down South, we say, "God gave you two ears and one mouth." There's a reason behind it, so I started listening a little bit more and paying attention to the old cliché that there are always two sides to every story. This prepared me to be more open to paying attention to more of what I was taught than what I was fed.

When you listen to someone, you also learn about their morals, ethics, business philosophies, and listening tells you who to stay away from. It's okay if you make a bad mistake and you stay too near to someone for a portion of time, as long as you remember to use your two ears. At some point, you will see that those people aren't worth your time. They aren't worth your thoughts, your tears, your happiness, or anything else. You need to stay away from them.

Sure, I cry at sad movies, and an animal in pain does something to me. But humans have a choice. And some humans, I just have no use for. One of my sayings is that "Certain people are just a waste of breathing air." People who want to do harm, be it physical, mental, or those who play games...well, I just have no use for them.

At this point in my life, I've gotten to where I can read people pretty well. And I will do anything for the people I am closest to. I will take a bullet in a heartbeat for Brian Stevens. That guy's so real, and genuine that he is family to me.

So, I'm guarded on some matters, and people who are overly dramatic turn me off. I actually find them pathetic and disgusting and try to stay away from people like that. I don't mean people who have a genuine reason to be upset, but I'm talking about people who try and milk their situations.

If you ever talk to somebody who I don't like, they'll probably all tell you the same thing. I don't pay attention. I don't even look at them. I ignore them and walk away. I have no tolerance for it. If I like you; I'll take a bullet for you. But if you mean nothing to me, I walk away.

My parents were each married and divorced numerous times, and I would say my attitude has something to do with how I treat people. And I especially can't stand fake people. Since I can remember, even when I was a little kid, the people who would come up and pinch my cheeks at four years old drove me f*cking insane.

When I was 11, my mom worked at a fine ladies' apparel shop. My parents had divorced by then, and my mom's co-worker would come up to me with this horrible, gruesome smile and tell me how she'd missed me so much in the two weeks that I hadn't been at the store. It turned my stomach. I thought *you don't know me. You don't even know my name.*

I had a real hard time with religion also. We changed churches and religions like most people change underwear. I've been Baptist, Methodist, Mormon, and in every kind of Christianity under the sun. I think of organized religion like organized crime.

This is why I'm very much a fan of the spiritual angle. There's something bigger out there. We're not sitting here by accident, and I certainly don't believe in evolution. But organized religion drives me insane.

Even though my parents divorced, my dad remained my best friend. I absolutely adored my father. The two people in my life who were the beacons I used to guide my path were my maternal grandfather and my father. My father was my buddy. Since my parents divorced when I was 11, my brother and I lived with my dad from that point until I was out of the house. Part of the reason I was so close to my dad was because he was that guy who never had a bad day. He was happy every single day. He was very positive and a hard worker. He had a great work ethic from working as a supervising mechanic at Maxwell House from the time he was in his early 20s.

After Maxwell House, he transferred to Ingersoll Rand/Dresser Rand Industries, where he was a factory service rep. He was a long-haired, tattooed biker, who always had a good day. Every person that I ever introduced to my dad loved him. He was responsible like an adult but had a childlike heart.

My dad spoke his mind. He was never afraid of what somebody else thought or said, but he was also the kindest, most gentle human being that you'd ever run across. I am very proud that he was my father. He was my best friend for years in life, gave me a lot of good life lessons, but for some stupid reason; I didn't start listening to him until I was 21.

Before he passed away, I got to tell him that when I was a teenager, I was amazed at how stupid he was, but when I turned 21 years old, it was incredible how smart he got overnight. If you're about my age, you'll understand exactly what that means. He was always an intelligent man. I was just a young, dumb high school kid who "knew" everything and assumed parents had no idea what they were talking about.

My dad worked very hard his whole life. He was not afraid of work. Seven days a week, 12 hours a day, and often, 16 hours a day. He busted his ass, and always made sure we had food and that we were taken care of. It was important to him. But he also had a laid-back type of personality. He enjoyed his friends. He would go out and party, sure, but he was still up at 6:00 AM for work every single day.

My brother and I always make a joke about the movie, *Apollo 13*. When the astronauts were running out of oxygen, and they were getting ready to pass away, they threw all those parts on the table to the group of engineers saying, in essence, "We need to make this work." That was my father. My father could do what no one else in the world could do. People all over this country, and all over this globe, relied on him in his profession. They would actually call and ask for him by name to keep their companies, chemical plants, oilfields, and refineries, up and running.

He was by far, one of the greatest in his field, as he progressed through life, and I was a lucky man.

My mom will tell you that I raised my dad to the ripe old age of 18 and that he never got past 18, even up until the day before he was killed.

I had called him up and asked for help rebuilding my bathroom, and he was there like that. We spent the whole day together, the day before he got killed. I think I knew that day, that it was going to be the last day I'd ever see him because when I hugged him goodbye that evening when he left to go back home, I held him a little tighter than I ever had. I remember smelling him a little deeper than I ever had, and I helped him turn his motorcycle around. He was very able-bodied, but I think I knew at that moment it would be the last time I would ever see him again.

The day he died, he was leaving an ice house and was on a private road. In Texas, we call the roads that run beside the freeway, feeder roads.

This particular feeder road was a two-way. Since then they've changed it, and it's been turned into a single lane. He was pulling out and turning left, which was west. A car turning south had stopped and then was going to proceed.

My dad had pulled out into his lane of traffic and made it about 30 or 40 feet when a guy in an F-350 Ford pickup with a big ranch hand bumper on the front, decided that he didn't want to wait for that car to turn. He moved into the lane of oncoming traffic going somewhere between 80 and 100 miles an hour and hit my father head-on while he was on the motorcycle. He hit my father so hard that my father, who weighed 188 pounds, flew 69 yards. His motorcycle flew 83 yards. Think about this. A 1,000-pound Harley Davidson Road King flew 83 yards.

Then the guy tried to run. He went through the grassy median in the middle, sped onto the freeway and totaled two or three cars before flipping his truck. In Texas—just as it is in most places--it's okay to kill a biker. So, this guy didn't spend one day in jail, and no charges were pressed. This man took my father, John Wayne (Taco) Fowler away from us on January 3rd, 2010 at 5:56 PM because he was in too much of a hurry.

My stepmom called me up that night and asked if I knew where my dad was, and I said no, I hadn't heard from him. I knew he was going to New Orleans, but I hadn't heard from him. She said he hadn't been home to get his clothes. She said he hadn't even packed anything and so, she was really worried. I called my brother who lived far Northwest of Houston. At the time, I was living close to downtown Houston, and we headed toward my dad's house to see if maybe he had broken down on the side of the road. I ended up driving up on the accident.

It had happened at 5:56 PM on a Sunday, as I mentioned, and at 10 o'clock that night he was still there. I could see the accident ahead of me, and when I drove up on it, I found out what had happened to him. Then, I called the rest of my family and let them know. I was the executor of his will, and so I had to tell everyone what had happened.

I also had to get all the death certificates and cancel all his accounts as well as sell his house.

It was definitely the worst day of my life. My dad and I were exactly 20 years apart, and I had just turned 40. The accident happened on January 3rd, meaning I was four months into being 40, and he was going to be 61 on March 15th.

I take after him in one way or another. The running joke has always been that I was born in the hospital and brought home in a saddlebag on a motorcycle.

I don't think that's true. I think I was born in a hospital and came home in a Ford Torino GT convertible if I remember the stories correctly. My father drove that after his '55 Chevy. So, I was born into cars. I had no choice. But the motorcycle legacy is true. I got my first motorcycle when I was just 15 years old. And from that point forward, I always had motorcycles until I had to give them up. Motorcycles were an important part of my life. I've taken motorcycle trips through New England, on the way to Laconia Bike Week. I've ridden through the middle of the country, on my way to Sturgis, South Dakota. I've cruised through North Dakota, Montana, Idaho, Wyoming, and Colorado, and been up and down California. I've covered the four corners, Nevada, Utah, Arizona, New Mexico, and been all over Florida. I've always enjoyed riding. It's a pastime and passion.

Since my father was killed on his motorcycle, my family made it very difficult for me to remain a motorcycle rider.

45

They wanted me to get rid of my bikes. My wife worried, and I can understand that. It makes all the sense in the world. My brother and mother felt the same way. I kept my motorcycles up until New Year's Eve of 2015 when I sold the last one. I had bought a Harley Ultra Classic, commonly referred to as a Geezer Glide. It was a wonderful, incredible motorcycle. The one I had before that was a Street Glide. I remember taking trips on both of them. I put so many miles on that Street Glide.

But I had to listen to my family and hear their concerns and even though today it stings that I don't ride, it was a better choice, so my family could sleep at night, so my family could know that I was coming home, rather than indulging in riding. But I will always be a fan. I'll always be a biker. It's been born and bred into me. It gives me the clarity and understanding that there is a much larger power than us. As you're riding through the mountains, listening to chamber music, and taking in the scenery, you recognize how small you are on this great big globe, and how really insignificant and important we can be at the same time. When you ride, you will see it; you will feel it. I highly recommend that you get on the back of any motorcycle if you're too afraid to drive one. Any good biker will take you anywhere you want to go so you can feel the spiritual moment of realizing who you are on this miraculous planet.

As you're riding through the mountains, you'll look over to see a lake on your left-hand side and then buffalo, or deer, antelope, or elk, on your right-hand side. Up ahead of you are curves. Behind you are curves. Above you are blue skies as brilliant as you could ever imagine. You've got your friends and your family with you and riding is just one of the most magnificent things that God's ever given us. One of my fondest moments on a motorcycle came to me about six years ago. My next-door neighbor, Conda Maze, asked me if I would take his mother on a motorcycle ride for her 80th birthday. When they helped her on the back of my motorcycle, we drove through the neighborhood at a good six or seven miles an hour. The appreciation and honor of somebody asking me to take their mother on her 80th birthday, for a motorcycle ride, is a memory I'll take with me forever.

Because of my dad, I never realized we were poor growing up because I had everything that I needed. We never went a day without a meal. We did have to steal electricity a couple of times from the neighbors, but we had a good life. I can think back to one clue that might've given away our lifestyle—that my wife caringly teases me about. When I was in junior high, I had one pair of jeans.

Every day, I would come home from school and would wash that one pair of jeans, and make sure that I had clean jeans for the next day. I had one pair of shoes, too, and when the holes busted through the bottom, I would put tape inside of them. When the laces busted, I would take laces from other shoes, to fix them. So, while we were loved and taken care of, we didn't have everything that other kids had. To this day, if you go in my closet, if there are less than 40 pairs of jeans in there, something's wrong.

I own probably seven pairs of the same exact shoe. I own four pairs of the same exact cowboy boot. I always said, "When I make it, I'm going to have seven pairs of jeans. I'm going to have a different pair of jeans for every day of the week." Probably ever since that first year when I made a hundred grand, I always made sure that I never ran out of jeans.

Chapter 3: If You Can Do It Better, Do It

"Everyone can tell you the risk. An entrepreneur can see the reward." ~Robert Kiyosaki

In 1994, I financed my first house. I had a condo before that but didn't really finance it. So, this house was truly the first place I consider my own. I bought it for $72,900, and I knew that I could never pay the f*cking note. It was $800 a month. My interest rate was 8.5%. But I started doing mortgage loans because I'd had a horrible experience buying that dang house. My loan officer sucked. I met and talked to him once; otherwise, his customer service skills were nonexistent.

Then I talked to a processor. This girl called me every freaking day asking for something different. She called me on Monday asking for a paycheck stub, Tuesday, asking for a tax return, Wednesday asking for something completely f*cking different. I got mad at her and said, "You've gotta be kidding me; there has to be a better way to do this. Do you not have a list of everything that you need so I can get it all at once?" And she said—now, remember, she's the reason I'm in the mortgage business today—"Well if you think you can do it better, why don't you?" In fact, it feels like this is a theme to my life.

That was all I needed to hear. I signed up to take classes on mortgage origination, and I took a broker class from an independent broker. That class cost me $500, and I took it right before I'd closed and financed my first house. I met a broker there, and he let me work for him, and so I did that part-time while I continued to work in the oilfield. The oilfield had slowed down by then, and I was making about $75,000 a year. So, when I started earning that same amount in the mortgage business, I planned to quit the oilfield business.

What I didn't think about is, when you're making $75,000 in the oilfield and $75,000 in the mortgage business, you're truly making $150,000 a year, but you're also spending $150,000 a year. That meant I was not just changing jobs; I was cutting my salary in half.

After I had that realization, the next day on my way into work, I called my girlfriend, who's my wife now, and said, "I can't do this one more day. I cannot work for these people. I cannot work in this business one more second. When you get to work today will you please write up my resignation letter because I'm quitting today?"

She gave me the typical bit of, "Oh my God, what are we going to do?" I answered: "I've got about $50,000 saved up and I'm going into the mortgage business full-time. I'm going to chance it, and if I fall on my face, I can always go back to this crap. But I'm just not going to do this one more f*cking day. I hate these people. I hate this company."

I had had it with working for somebody's brother-in-law or relative who knows nothing, as had seemed to be the case for most of my life. It was infuriating. There are a lot of really good people in the business. Some of them are still there, but given the chance, I think every one of them would leave because it's such a crazy, boring business.

Even though I had chopped my earnings in half, I had carried a $2M pipeline, although I didn't have a license until 1999. With no requirement to hold a mortgage license, anyone could process a mortgage. That was my plan.

At the start of running this new business, I was terrified but made sure I remembered my standards for how I wanted my company to run. You can learn all about them in Section II of the book when I talk all about minding your business.

Chapter 4: Grit, Hustle, Love

"On a mission to build an empire and leave a legacy."

~Rachel Ngom

In the first days, weeks and months of the business, I looked at my bank account every day, and I would count down from $50K to $47K. Then from $47K to $45K and then $42K. Every single day, I was like, "Oh sh*t, oh sh*t, oh sh*t, oh sh*t, oh sh*t." But at the same time, I also had to be positive; I had to keep my smile on and let everybody know that everything was okay. I was a duck, paddling my ass off underwater even though everyone saw me as being smooth and pretty on top. I had no idea what I was doing.

Daily, I thought *what have I done?* I knew that there were 50 things that I was supposed to do, but I didn't know where to start.

I'm not a big planner. If you're a believer of the Personalysis Test, I'm a high red. On a scale of zero to 6.5, I'm a 6.5 red. What that means is that I ask forgiveness instead of permission.

So, I didn't use a whiteboard. I didn't identify tasks or organize. I just knew I had to go make money.

That meant *not* doing it on the phone.

One of my great friends, Chad Prior, uses the tagline: Imperfect Action Takers. I think it's one of the greatest taglines that's ever been introduced to humankind because taking imperfect action, simply doing something, and not coming up with excuses is powerful. It's not hard. In fact, it's easy. All you have to do is just do something positive. Do something for yourself. Do something for your family. Get up off your ass and do something. Don't sit back in the f*cking lazy chair and bitch about life. You've got to be positive even when what's happening in your life feels negative. That doesn't matter. You've got to look past it. I get so sick of listening to people whine and bitch about how life or somebody has done them wrong.

Someone told me a long time ago that there's not a whole lot of difference between a person who has nothing and a person who has millions except for the fact that the person who has millions did something. They got up off their ass.

Compare two people who were both born in the same country, state, area, and maybe even year. The difference between the successful one and the unsuccessful one is that the successful one got up off their ass and took action.

I had to take imperfect action, and besides, I'm strange on the phone. I have to have a headset, and I need 1,000-square feet or more, so I can walk around. Even dictating this book right now and sitting in one spot is really hard for me.

When I walk, I talk; I wring my hands and am very physical.

So, instead of calling, I got in my truck and made sales calls to real estate offices, before realizing that was probably one of the dumbest things I could do.

Who the hell are you to go into an office unannounced, bringing zero value and begging for business while you insist that "I'll try really hard," or "I'm better than anybody else." You don't know that you're better than anybody else. Usually, mortgage guys do nothing but take from real estate agents.

That's one of the reasons we're on our way to Duluth, Minnesota right now, to train 50 real estate agents on how to get more business. It's because we want to bring them something of value. We're teaching them; we're giving to them because most real estate people never went to school to learn how to sell. They were taught how to fill out a contract; they were taught how to stay out of jail; they were taught how not to get their license taken away. So, they have to rely on somebody else to teach them how to sell. Screw these coaches charging tens of thousands of dollars if not $50K to teach a realtor how to sell. I'd rather bring knowledge that realtors can use today, right now. And when they do, they make themselves feel good because they just sold something. They did what they got their license to do. I've focused on giving back to realtors for years now.

Even in those early years, I wondered how I could give back (when I got my feet under me).

When the crash came and upended the industry, Cassy and I were navigating the marriage waters and running into our own rough patch.

I didn't know the whole of what was going on in the market, but I knew I had to fix it. At the time I had about 5,000 loan officers, and 700 offices in 50 states. Knowing I had to fix what was wrong caused a lot of problems. I can look back and prove that the joke about youth being wasted on the young is true.

But before you get too attached to that idea, I also get pissed off at the fact that wisdom can be wasted on the old. It took me this many years to figure out what the f*ck is going on in life and why. It took me this long to learn to stay in my lane and control what I can control, to worry about my own sh*t. I see a lot of people get out of their lane. They work on what has nothing to do with them. They waste time and money on people who don't deserve it.

They're stealing it. You're wasting your time. You're killing yourself, and it makes absolutely no sense.

Cas and I divorced in 2007, got back together in 2010 after my father was killed and remarried in 2012. We will be and have been married forever. We make the joke to each other: "I wanted half of my sh*t back." She has always had my back, and I will always have hers.

With Cassy's support in 1999, I joined Acme Home Mortgage with the aim to help them grow their business even though I was scared sh*tless.

Cassy had a young daughter at the time, and by now, she is my daughter, too, since I have known her over 20 years. Amanda was four years old when she and Cassy moved in with me. I shared responsibility for her, and I had the realization that it's not just me anymore who needs to be taken care of because I could fail and sleep on my dad's couch. Now, I had not only a wife, but I was responsible for a four-year-old little one who not only doesn't know what it means to worry about the budget and providing, but she shouldn't know. She should have a fairytale childhood.

When I met Cassy, it was 1998, and I was still working in the oilfield and doing mortgages on the side. I was the foreman at a shop in Houston, and so, I was in charge of everything out in the repair center. When a delivery guy was sick one day, I had to pick up parts from a machine shop. So, I went over to the shop, which was owned by my buddy.

When I opened the door and walked in, I experienced an absolutely perfect moment. It had to have been in the afternoon because when I swung open the door, the sunshine was behind me and it just lit Cassy up. She was the office manager at this machine shop.

Right in front of me was this beautiful blonde-haired, tan-skinned, in-a-cute-sundress, girl sitting at the front desk. I asked to see my buddy, Bill. She wanted to know who I was. I thought she was flirting with me, but I wasn't really good at translating those signals, so I didn't know exactly if she was flirting with me or if she had gas.

Anyway, she went and got Bill. After that, I started going over there to drop stuff off and pick stuff up instead of sending Travis, my driver.

In the meantime, Bill, who owned the shop, kept hinting to Cassy that she should go out with me. Cassy repeatedly said no. Then Bill finally said, "Why won't you go out with

Jonny?" Now, at this time, I didn't know those two were talking about me. He hadn't said anything, and neither had she. Sure, she had flirted with me a little bit. But I acted like a stupid boy. I just went over there, thinking *she's flirting with me.*

When Bill, my buddy, told me I should ask her out, I hesitated. "Ah, man, I don't know." Come to find out the reason that she kept telling Bill that she wouldn't go out with me was because she was a single mom and she thought I was the truck driver. She knew there was no way that a truck driver was going to be able to support her and her baby!

That gets me laughing, and now, I use what she said against her all the time. "You were so shallow." I poke fun at her. She'll protest, "No, I was being honest. If you were making eight bucks an hour how could you even think about supporting me and my baby?" I just tell her, "I understand that; it makes sense. Whatever. Gold digger."

Bill proceeded to tell her, "No, no, baby, he runs that whole f*cking shop over there for Dresser Industries. He's making good money." I don't remember how I got her number, but I started calling and talking to her. So, I asked her out, and she said, "Oh, nah, I don't think so. I can't do that." Now, I'm thinking *you've got to be f*cking kidding me. What is this a setup? Why is my buddy telling me to go for it and she's flirting with me but turning me down?*

The third time, when I asked her out, and she turned me down, I said, "I'm done. I'm not calling you anymore. I'm not coming over to your shop anymore. I'm not doing this sh*t. It's stupid." Then she told me well, she kind of had a boyfriend. And I said, "How can you *kind of* have a boyfriend?" She said, "We go out sometimes, but he lives on the other side of town, and I don't know if we're together right now or not." I told her "Well, that's a pretty simple one. If he's not nice to you and he doesn't do anything for you, then f*cking dump his ass." She said, "I don't know. I can't do that." So, I hung up. I was done. Then within about two or three hours she called me up and said, "Alright, I told him we were done. I broke up with him. Do you still want to go out tonight?" I said, "Yes," If I ever saw her again, I didn't give a damn, but I took her answer as a victory.

It was August 8, 1998. I was nervous as f*ck. I picked her up, and we went out to this fancy seafood place. Then we ended up going over to a friend of hers. I truly was just enamored with her.

We were never really separated again for years after that unless I had to go out of town. Our first date was on August 8, 1998, and my birthday was on August 12th. We had only been seeing each other for four days even though we had known of each other for months. Still, Cassy and my mom surprised me at work and brought me a birthday cake.

Here's a funny twist to that story. The guy who was *kind of* her boyfriend and wasn't very nice to her, worked at the same place as she did. He was friends with Bill also.

At the beginning of October my buddy, her boss, fired her because her dating me and not being with her ex anymore caused too much disruption in their place of business. I was done with "my buddy" then. It was a scumbag choice to make. *You're the f*cking a**hole who pushed her to go out with me, and she is a single mom. You're firing her because she did what you persuaded her to do?*

She was without a job for 24-48 hours before customers of hers reached out to her on her cell phone. All these different companies wanted her to work for them. One of those companies was called Valves Incorporated They called her two days after she got fired; she interviewed with them and was immediately hired. This October will be her 20th year with them.

She started as their office manager answering the phones, setting appointments, talking to customers, and doing other admin/customer service work for $10 an hour. Now, after working her way up every single day, she is a female running the inside sales division. She sells more and has created more revenue for that company than any other salesperson inside or outside.

She runs the repair facility where there are a dozen guys, and she is the one girl out there working in the repair department. Cassy's an absolute powerhouse. But one thing I can warn you about is that people who have that much tenacity and drive can also be a real pain in the ass to live with sometimes. So, everything is not always roses;

there's always a downside but that's marriage, and that's life, and it's pretty damn great.

We got married in Jamaica, and sure, we had some problems that were coming from both sides. One of the biggest issues cropped up when the mortgage crash happened as I said earlier. I'm a fixer; I make things happen. I either get things done, or I think about how I'm going to get things done. Getting my arms around the crash and the challenges in my marriage required making plans.

When the crash happened, I was a loan officer with my own branch, mostly working as a banker as opposed to a broker. Acme Home Mortgage lost their name in court to a lender out of FLA who wound up changing it. At the end of 2000. I complained to the owner because they weren't doing what they were supposed to. Rent was not getting paid on time, and some major responsibilities were being ignored. When I pointed this out to the owner of the company, he said, "If you think you can do it better, do it."

When I had first taken the job with Acme, I had been offered a base and commission override and more money than I could ever imagine: a $50K base with 10 basis points for every branch for a year. When I took this job, the top performing-branch of the company was doing about $11M per month. I calculated if I brought that branch on, I would pull in $11K. It was more money than a broke d*ck kid from the oilfields had ever made. But after 2-3 weeks, I was miserable having gone from running my own shop to having to be somewhere at 9 AM. I dealt with 2-3 recruiters and 4-5 customer service branch coordinators. I started in June and did not take a commission check for six months. Then in December 2009, my first commission check was $23,000, which was at that time, the largest commission check I had ever received. But as times went by I learned words didn't mean sh*t. The guys I was working with had no morals or ethics. It was a case of "contracts were made to be broken."

In my second month, I was sent in a truck to pick up a motorcycle trailer from a guy my boss had sued. He had sued for a low-seven-figure and settled out of court for the motorcycle trailer. At the time I thought, *when you are making $20K-40K a month, you are the smartest person in the world.*

Here's a spoiler alert and a life lesson you can't ignore. You aren't the smartest person even if you think you must be. When I started making too much money, the company thanked me by cutting my commission five times. The original agreement had been that I would make $50K per year with 10 basis points per month for one year of production. Then those points were slashed to five basis points for the first six months, and two basis points for the next six months. Then it was changed again to three basis points for one year. My points were adjusted one last time to three basis points for six months. While this was going on, I still had to keep people happy. It was my job to come up with newer, easier and faster—no matter the subject or objective. I had built a trigger lead, and we were using millions of trigger leads per year.

I busted my ass for the first eight months, seven days a week, 16 hours a day. In February of 2000, I hit $100M, and the owner of the company said he thought that would have never been possible. I did it in eight months.

Along about 2005, the owner of the company and I were sitting outside on a restaurant patio, when I asked him what the most money he had ever made in a year was. He looked at me and said, "That reminds me. I never thanked you." Then he rattled off the fact the company had cleared $20M+ that year. As he was talking, I thought, *but you did cut my pay.*

I still did not quit. I had blind loyalty. Yes, I thought about calling it quits many times, but I remained with the company for a bit longer.

He made enough money that he bought a personal jet, and plane. He had a couple of hangers and a couple of houses down in the Virgin Islands. He had a couple of houses in Aspen, Sturgis, and in South Dakota as well. We would visit them, and it was kind of cool at the time. I never thought about that we were traveling around in a personal jet and going anyplace we wanted to go—whether we chose Fort Lauderdale for lunch, and then the Indy 500. Or, if we wanted to watch the U.S. Grand Prix or run up to Sturgis and take a quick motorcycle ride—we had that ability.

While I was sitting across the table from him and remembering all the trips we had taken, and what this guy who was supposed to be my friend was telling me about making more money than he thought possible, it was a defining moment of my life. I seethed inside again: *You cut my commission five times.* I also alternately seethed and laughed over his habit of hiring operations managers that were mostly short-timers. My boss was known around the office as always hiring the "flavor of the week." He would bring on people he didn't know and make them the operations manager. In a 10-year period, there were 27 underwriting managers.

I knew it was time to leave when the sh*t hit the fan in the form of another new hire. I met the guy and was told he was one of the three founders of Loans R Us, that he had sold all his stock and was looking for something to do. No due diligence was performed. Just like that, this guy was hired to run the whole company. Two weeks later we found out what a liar he was when the accounting department f*cked up my paycheck. I was supposed to have received $31,000 in commission and instead, got a check for $31.43. The owner decided the new guy could fix that problem and others. When the new guy got wind of how much the check was supposed to be he was shocked. He said he'd never seen that kind of money before. But he was supposedly one of the founders of Loans R Us—and at the time they were one of the largest lead providers in the country? It didn't make sense. He even remarked, "That's more money than I've ever made!"

In addition, I overheard conversations that he was plotting to get rid of me. That was the last straw.

I called my little brother who at the time was ranked #4 nationwide in a lead company. We did some digging and found out the new guy had been a salesman on the Loans R Us floor, who had gotten fired for lying to customers. The next day, I walked into our attorney's office, and told him that we had a problem. When I explained what was up and what I'd found out, his eyes grew to the size of frying pans. The expression on his face meant the new guy was busted. Just the day before he had bragged that he owned 179 rental properties after he had cashed out of Loans R Us.

Obviously, the new guy was a liar. He said he had an MBA from multiple universities in North Carolina, but it was all untrue, and the company knew, and the attorney knew. They had even given him a sign-on and moving bonus.

The company chose to handle this development by telling the guy they were having a hard time proving his background. They told him to go home, get his sheepskins and not to worry about coming back until he had the proof. Come to find out; he had also been an assistant manager at Kmart, who had been fired for stealing. Instead of being one of the founders at Loans R Us as he had told us, he was a salesperson.

We were brokering well over a billion and only banking $30M+ month. Translation: we were letting other companies do the greater amount of business than we were handling a month. To top it off, nearly 30 people were being given a new boss every 4-6 months. Something had to give.

Chapter 5: Adjusting Fire

"Home is where the waves crash." ~Unknown

We saw the crash, and the market changing in February of 2007. In my opinion, we noticed it long before the rest of the world, because we had such a large footprint, with so many people on the ground. So, you could watch, year over year, month over month, week over week and day over day, to gauge what the normal production was. When it started slowing down, we couldn't deny it. When you're doing that much business, and a shift of that magnitude in the market happens, it happens quickly. If you're doing a billion and a half dollars a month, and the next month, you drop by 10%, it means you've lost $150M in business in one month.

When you do that for two or three months, you cannot shrink fast enough to stay on top of the game because you still have staff to support. You are still a brand name that people are used to. This was an exceedingly difficult time.

We branched off to sell real estate franchises, and then created our own life insurance business, meaning, we had loan officers out selling life insurance. Looking back, this was part of our downfall. Not knowing what to expect was a great part of the mess, but we were also not taking care of what we were good at. We excelled in the mortgage business. We weren't good at ancillary issues that come up out of nowhere, and not surprisingly, it was turning people off.

For years and years, Joe, the owner played me like a puppet by insisting I provide him with client details. He didn't take the time to get to know his clients, so he relied on me to feed him facts about the people we worked with. When people walked up, I would whisper in Joe's ear, "This is so-and-so. They're from so-and-so. This is how much business they do." That way, he would know who it was. I was very, very familiar with every single person we had in the company. I'd personally brought most of them on, so I knew every branch manager, their spouses, and children, where they were, what they did, and I prided myself on having this information. I always found it kind of funny that I tried to help him remember names and facts. Then I got a chuckle out of the sheer fraudulent action of what he was doing, that he was pretending like he knew who these people were.

Joe and I were sometimes the best of friends as we ran the business, but other times, behind the scenes, and most every day, I argued with him, "Why the hell are we selling life insurance when we're good at the mortgage business? Why the hell are we selling real estate franchises when we're good at the mortgage business?"

That became a real problem between us, and we spent less time together—we stopped hanging out outside of work.

As time went on, and when I left the company, it became quite apparent that *there's something crazy here*. We were in more lawsuits than any dozen companies combined at any given time. It was just as much him, or the company, suing individuals, as it was companies who were suing us. I was told that this was normal, and not to be alarmed by it, so I didn't pay much attention to it after that.

Another odd event happened when he asked me if we could take my truck and go pick up some antiques that he had just bought. It was late in the afternoon. He and I got in my truck. We went over to the auction and picked up some pieces he had bought. Then he stopped for a minute to tell me a story about a time when he was a young man in business. As he tells it, he got called into the office because he was creating too much work for the administrative staff, underwriters, processors, closers, and everybody else since he was closing too many loans. So, they cut his comp in half, and told him if he worked twice as hard, he could make just as much money.

By this time, I had already had my comp cut five times, and I looked over at him, and said, "Do you realize that you've cut my pay five times since I've been working for you?" He became stone-faced, and said, "No, I did not." I had to refresh his memory that every time he got a new CFO, my pay was affected, that any time my check was over $30K, he had to cut my pay to put me in line because I was making too much money. There's a lesson from that. If you're in sales, and if you're the person bringing in the revenue to support the rest of the company, never put up with that BS.

There is another place you can go. You can even do it on your own. Any other company would be thrilled to death to have you, so never put up with somebody slapping a maximum amount on your value.

My last trip with him was in August of 2008. We would go to Sturgis every year, and in August of 2008, he had to terminate one of the branch managers who worked for us who had done a really lousy job. At the same time, with the crash, he could not shrink fast enough. He was losing six figures every month. I had caught onto what was happening in the market a year earlier, pointed it out, and then tried to explain and show Joe, what the facts were, but he wouldn't pay attention. Then as it got worse and worse and worse, he came to me and asked my advice. I suggested that we take our two top performing consultants and send them to Massachusetts to review the branch that was losing money, and then they could give their insight on what we could do to solve our problem. Actually, we needed to know if the problem could be fixed at all. In my opinion, these consultants failed because they said we were making the right decisions and going in the right direction. They said Joe could pull out of his situation. As history proved, that was completely inaccurate.

By the time we actually shut down that office, it had lost 7+ figures in 12 months from trying to keep the branch open. Now, while you're losing money in a crashing market, and you are paying gobs of money to keep a failing office open, well, that money has to come from somewhere, so one of the things that irritated me to death was the fact that we had to lay off key people in the corporate office. Other branches that were doing what they were supposed to do relied on these people, but these people lost their job because the guy sitting at the helm was either too blind or naïve to pay attention to what was going on with that one particular branch.

The branch was the largest office, but there were probably two or three dozen of similar size that were going into the negative rapidly. Because the owner was blinded to what was going on, people the producing branches relied on, were getting laid off as Joe made more decisions to slash jobs.

Round about November 1st of 2011 the feds shut down Acme. Acme fought for approximately six years, and Joe ended up owing somewhere around $300M for their fraudulent activities, but what was a shame about this part of my life—is that I had been there for 10 years by then. I'd built a good-sized company into becoming the number one independently owned powerhouse mortgage company. That made me proud, but to watch it fail needlessly was excruciating.

It was too much.

On May 1st, 2009, I could not take it one more day. Actually, the night before, I had gotten the strangest phone call from Joe asking me one of the dumbest questions I've ever been asked. In Texas, at the time we had what was called the CHL, Concealed Handgun License, and Texans think of it like the joke on *Miss Congeniality*, "It's Texas. Everyone carries a gun. My hairdresser carries a gun." That's the truth. My mother carries a gun.

Joe asked me, "Do you carry a gun?" I said, "That's a weird question. What do you mean?" He said that Shelly, his assistant had told him that I carried a gun. Most days, I did. I either had one on my hip or in my boot. I laughed it off and told him, "Well, sometimes I do. Sometimes I don't."

It was such a bizarre conversation, so I asked him, "Are you firing me?" He said, "No. I would never fire you." Then in the same breath, said, "I may have to let you off." I hung up the phone and laughed my ass off. Then I called a friend of mine who also worked for the company and told him the story. We both cracked up because Joe had just hired someone to replace me who was really, really bad. In a 10-year period, that was my first night of good sleep.

The next day was May 1st, and the end was imminent. I actually laughed about it when I went to lunch with my brother. When I got back to the office, Joe came down to see me, and we had a discussion. We both figured out it was time for me to leave. It was mutual. One of the telltale signs was that it was the first day I had felt like a real human being. I had talked to my mother that day and told her that I didn't work there anymore, and she said something that kicked me in the teeth: "I wish you would have left there two years ago, and I really wish you would have left five years ago." She didn't work with me. She didn't work for me. She had nothing to do with my business, but when my mother said I should have left so long ago it stung because she was right.

That day, I tried to give the people who worked for me direction, so they could manage themselves. I stayed until 7:00 that night, then I went home, and sat there with the biggest smile on my face. I was still making really good money, but even though I was walking away from it, it was one of the times in my life I knew I had made the healthiest decision for me. A lot of people would have freaked out if they had been in my shoes, but it was such a relief to have that piece of sh*t out of my life forever.

I took the month of May off and screwed around down in Florida for a couple weeks. Then I went to Manhattan for a week or two and didn't give a thought to work for the first time in an eternity.

Chapter 6: Men in Black

"Being sued by your own record company, that's even better than receiving a Grammy." ~Neil Young

After I left Acme, I connected with some local guys who are all very moral and ethical. While it initially wasn't a good fit to work with them, we did write an agreement because they wanted to grow and build a large mortgage company. My brother worked at that company, too, so these gentlemen and I talked a number of times, and I evaluated the situation to see if it was possible to join forces.

While I was checking out this new opportunity, I was still doing contract work for other mortgage companies. After a couple of months, the gentlemen and I decided that we could make an agreement work. It was going to take some doing and be a bit of a pain, but we would all concentrate on it. On December 31st, 2009 I became an employee.

It was me, my brother and four other partners in this agreement. From the very beginning, the agreement was, my brother and I were going to take an ownership piece. Then shortly after, a friend of mine who had been an attorney at Acme had had all he could take over there also. Then he was unable to join us likely due to client privilege and confidentiality. But I don't know because this person will never tell me the driving reason behind the conversation that we had when he pulled out of the agreement. I've never pried, but I can just imagine what he had seen and gone through. Eventually, he did end up working with us also.

It had been decided since one of the partners was leaving, that my brother and I, and our attorney were going to take his share, which was 25% of the company. The plan was to split that share up between the three of us. As we were building our company, and putting it together, my one-year non-compete, non-solicit agreement still had to be abided by, and I made sure I did. Come May 1, 2010—five months after my father was killed—we were open for business. We were going to take on the world.

Then another friend of mine, Linda Bullington, who happened to be with Joe's favorite branch, called me and told me she could not stay at that piece of sh*t company one more day. To hear that was unbelievable because she and her family were known as *the* mortgage hub in the city, since their hands were in a title company, too. So, any time the sh*t hit the fan, the whole family was in the middle of it.

According to Linda, there was no money to close loans. Traditionally, when you have a purchase money contract, on the day of closing, the new mortgage company pays off the old mortgage company. They take the lien and become the lien holder. Then they send a wire or a check to the title company to pay off the old lien. What was happening was, there was no money to pay off the old lien. The new mortgage company was not sending the money to pay off the old lien. According to Linda, she and her husband were playing what they called hat tricks.

For the hours or days that they waited on getting the money to fund the loan (that sometimes came, and sometimes didn't), Linda and her husband would have to invent stories on why the funding wasn't happening. Linda had had all she could take, and then she decided to join me. Her plan was to open up a branch and become an employee. By this time, we had already changed the company name. So, sometime in early June, Linda resigned and came on. This was my very first branch we'd opened. The date was June 9th, and by June 13th, when Linda resigned to Joe, he told her, "Good luck. Tell Jonny I said hello, and I'll start the lawsuit today."

On approximately June 13th Joe filed what's called the Texas 101 to sue me. He had no clue *why* he was suing me, but he was *going* to teach me a lesson. He was *going* to squash this kid who thought he could play in his game. This lawsuit went on for almost a year and a half, and it cost hundreds of thousands of dollars. Joe had transformed into a bully trying to beat someone up on the playground.

The only difference is, this time, the person on the playground didn't back down. I had exceptional people backing me, and I was not going to tolerate his mistreatment. Nobody had ever stood up to Joe before. Luckily, we had the greatest lawyers that walked the Earth and who were on our side. My lawyers beat his lawyer's ass every single day.

This experience taught me a lot more than I ever wanted to learn about the legal system. I still have lawyers calling and asking me about it. They want to know: "How did this happen?" We went through more depositions than I can remember. More lies were told about me by people who I thought were my friends, and they made these decisions just to protect themselves and the company. I lost a lot of friends. I also discovered who my friends and frenemies were.

Whoever told you the justice system was just lied to you. They have no f*cking clue what they're talking about, because there is nothing just about our justice system, and there is nothing legal about our legal system. I don't give a f*ck what anybody says or thinks because I can prove it to them all day long. What's real is, whoever has the most money wins.

When you are involved in a lawsuit, you will encounter a lot of highly educated people who use very large words that few people know the meaning of. These lawyers like making you feel smaller. Don't ever let them control you during this process. That's another failure of the justice system. I agree that attorneys need to go to school. I agree they need to know the law. But at some point, they need to stop acting like prima donnas and communicate with the common public because, unless you have a law degree, you probably won't understand at least half of their terminology. Yet these morons have the ability to ask you if you understand, and if you don't nod yes or say yes, well, then, you're the only one in the room who doesn't understand.

Hundreds of thousands of dollars in depositions and umpteenth amended petitions were racked up, including the last one controlling the use of the intellectual properties I had gained over a 10-year period. Not that I would have acted inappropriately or illegally. Joe's attorneys were known as sports litigators. Meaning, anyone can file a lawsuit on anyone for anything, and it doesn't have to be true. So, he and his attorneys would change or redirect the lawsuit to keep it going, for sport. They attempted to sue for one reason and then would ask a barrage of questions, so the answers to those questions could fuel another frivolous lawsuit. They would file an amendment for not doing due diligence and not checking the name of a client, for example. Then they would argue that not doing the due diligence would expose Joe to risk. The idea of this sport litigation is to smash and break the other party. Joe's behavior allowed by the court and ruled by a piss-poor judge—led to the feds suing him and his other crooked cronies.

The judge behaved so poorly, playing solitaire through most of the trial. At any time, that I was on the stand, I could look over at his computers and see he was playing games and not paying attention. His behavior is pretty standard for our legal system. People might suggest that I could go back and read the notes or listen to the court recordings to see if what I saw was true, but I call bullsh*t. I know this guy was playing computer games because I watched him.

Each deposition can cost up to $10,000. You're paying for your attorney. You're paying for a room. You're paying for a court reporter. In my case, you're paying for a videographer, which is extremely expensive. And the purpose of these depositions is simply to bully you around and show you who the boss is because, after about one or two depositions, you can't afford to fight anymore.

Joe and his lawyer went for the jugular as much as possible, scraping and searching my Facebook page and using what other people who were on Acme's side had posted on my page. I found it hilarious because I hadn't written about what they had accused me of even though they were intent on calling me out for it. Knowing where I am today, and that in some circles people call me a social media expert and realizing that people were trying to string me up with content I hadn't written and didn't engage in, is ludicrous. The premise was the fact the posts were on my wall at all, meant I had been complicit. At the time the whole drama was playing out, and I was falsely accused, it was amusing.

I told my legal team numerous times, "Just let me quit. Let me leave the business. Let me go work at Home Depot until he goes away," but they wouldn't let me. They refused. I even said multiple times because I was living paycheck to paycheck, "Let me give you my Harley." I just wanted the drama and torture to end. I was struggling to get by while also going to court numerous times a week, enduring multiple depositions.

At one point, I remember hearing one of the court clerks reference the amount of paperwork in the case, that it looked like GE and Wal-Mart had locked horns in litigation against each other. It was that overwhelming. For some reason, Joe just wanted to teach me who the boss was, so he just kept foolishly throwing money at his lawyers.

Very few people ever get to see karma. But I had a front-row seat to the greatest karma concert ever played in history when I was called to attend a federal deposition as a witness. Every time I gave them the information they'd asked for, within a day or two I had another deposition to attend to testify in the case against me. I would sit in these depositions with the biggest grin on my face not because of what was going on at the time during my deposition, but for a simpler reason. I knew what they didn't. The company was getting shut down. They were at the mercy of a federal indictment, and I was helping to put this despicable human out of business. The bonus was that he knew nothing about it.

Dealing with the feds taught me that every fed has the same first name. It's Special Agent. They all wear the same black suit and black glasses. It is very ominous. After you go through a number of metal and bomb detectors and you walk by the dogs, you're escorted into an amazing room with enormous flat-screen television panels on the wall. While the Department of Justice sat in New York City, I sat in Austin, Texas, with at least one court reporter, as well as two special agents, and my attorney.

At some point, I learned a really cool fact about myself after having every grain of dirt dug up on me. I don't remember if I read this new information or heard it over the phone, but the Department of Justice told my attorney that not only was I *not* a target for any investigation but that I was a very, very, very good guy.

The phrase "People who live in glass houses should not throw rocks" comes to mind during this time in my life. If you can withstand the stones, then you have nothing to worry about. Hearing I was seen as a good guy, filled me with pride.

It made a really glorious day for me every single time I was called to depose. It wasn't only me who was delighted at this turn; there were somewhere between six and 12 other people Joe was suing at the same time for frivolous crap that the courts allow. These people also became federal witnesses, and they were more than happy to answer any questions in these federal depositions. It was a fantastic feeling for those of us who had been picked on and beat up by a sport-litigating bully, and we went to bed every night with a smile on our faces. Just knowing that this man was going to spend his golden years in misery was worth it.

By this time, we were already hundreds of thousands of dollars into this suit, and everyone who was involved in fighting him, just couldn't let it go. We agreed if he paid us $250,000, that we would all walk away. The reason we came up with the $250,000 is that is approximately what we had spent up to that point.

On November 1st, 2011, the feds shut down Acme Home Mortgage. Branches left in droves. They pulled his agency tickets and ability to do FHA and VA loans, which is why I love this date. But, of course, he had protected his interests. If Acme went out of business, there was AcmeQuest Mortgage and AcmeQuest Home Mortgage Limited and even more mortgage companies that he would just open up.

We made the offer to get out of the lawsuit for $250,000.

Then Joe announced that "Jonny offered to not let this happen for $250,000. In hindsight, I guess I should have taken it." My understanding and the feds' understanding was that he was trying to make it look like *I* was shutting him down, not the feds and that *I* was trying to extort $250,000.

My court date for my pretrial was the Tuesday before Thanksgiving. In the pretrial, you sit in a courtroom with a judge and the lawyers argue about what's going to be shown and what's not going to be shown, what's going to be discussed and what's not going to be discussed, and so forth.

We bided our time in the courtroom all day long, and I sat in the background with the largest smile on my face (thank God, I'd had braces, so every tooth in my head was showing). After eight or nine hours, I watched the same judge that I couldn't stand, find in our favor on what would be allowed. At one point, I laughed so hard the judge shot me a warning look to zip it. Joe's three attorneys were seated on one side of the table, and my attorneys were on the other. One of his little bitty midget attorneys turned and mouthed the words, "What the f*ck?" to someone close to her. That's how bad they were getting their asses kicked all day long in pretrial.

That afternoon, I looked at my attorney, who was one of the greatest litigators I have ever had the pleasure of seeing in action. His name is Paul Methuselah, and I will always be forever grateful to him because he was the baddest son of a bitch in town. He put every single one of those attorneys in their place. I told Paul, "After all of this time going through this, they're going to file a nonsuit tomorrow, I promise you." Paul said he wasn't sure if that was going to happen, but it was very possible. I was convinced it was a huge possibility because they'd had their ass pummeled. The judge rejected everything they tried to throw out and accepted everything they disallowed.

I got the news about 9:00 in the morning on the Wednesday before the Thanksgiving of 2011 that they had filed nonsuit. In case you're unfamiliar, nonsuit means, that after these sharks had wasted money, time, my life, dozens and dozens of other people's time and lives, they filed a piece of paper that said, they had changed their mind. Now, all of a sudden, they were not going to sue me. Doing this permitted them to walk away.

What this grueling experience takes from your mind, and your body, and what it takes off your years is irreplaceable. You can never, ever replace that time and frustration. You can never replace going home every single day, having to plaster on a happy face for your family after you've just been through eight hours of questioning or eight hours of court or enduring a temporary restraining order. You will never get back what you've lost. My advice to anybody is, if you're going through this, learn. Listen. Pay attention. Realize you're in charge because people, for the most part, are not in charge. It's a circus, and you've got to remember what you're there for. You have to keep pushing forward.

Also, and maybe this is obvious, stay out of lawsuits as much as you can. Nobody wins except for the attorneys. Tell the truth. The truth is so much easier to remember. I've never been good at lying, so I was safe throughout the whole proceeding. Then keep your eyes and ears open and your mouth shut. Look at who surrounds you. Listen to who says they're your friend, and make sure that's accurate. Maybe even test people. Do what I did and give out erroneous information to people to see if they're telling the truth, to see if they're your friends, or if they're dense enough to blurt out what you have said to set them up. That actually happened in my case.

Before you get to the point where you think court is necessary, you may want to reach out to somebody who's been through it and ask them about their experiences. Before you ever put down that first retainer or accept being sued and think you're going to win, tread carefully because you might not.

Now, at least, I'm prepared if it ever happens again, and I know how to work the inside of the system. Because of this knowledge, God forbid I find myself sitting in a courtroom again, I have confidence I will be better prepared and smarter than anybody on the opposing side.

One of the components that make our justice system an absolute joke is that after you file your nonsuit, you can walk away. You can literally change your mind. If you know you're going to lose, and if your company no longer exists, then it doesn't matter, because there's nothing to go after any more.

Chapter 7: Leading Myself

"Always deliver more than expected." ~Larry Page

While my ass was getting dragged in court, I was still in the process of building my new business and training our new staff.

We were dealing with a lot of people, and for me to be at my peak, I have to know exactly who my customer is, so I can work authentically with that person.

I worked on my business every spare moment I could and before I knew it, six years had passed. I made sure every day that I worked in my new passion that I never forgot to apply what I had learned from Joe and his insane obsession with taking me to court. I needed never to find myself in that predicament again.

As I grew more detached from what had happened, I instilled many other values in my company. For instance, I want my company to have interchangeable worth. I joke that in theory, you could take Steve Brand, pull him out of Minnesota, and put him in Tennessee in Alex Jimenez's office and the business would run exactly the same. That's what I mean by needing to know who our customer is.

There may be a few small differences, of course. One person may be into technology more than the other, but ideally, each office should run exactly the same. The goal is for the customers to only see a different face. These are the kind of people I like working with. I've gotten to a point in my life where I refuse to work with anybody I don't like because it causes more problems than it brings value. The reality is any one of these guys can work anywhere, and anyone would be thrilled to have them on their team.

The problem is most companies don't realize the company is the servant and the branch manager is the customer. They try and mash their people into a box they don't fit in. Instead of helping, enhancing and bringing value, they try to change the way that they do business.

Take Steve. He wears a T-shirt, shorts and tennis shoes. In some of these more conservative and bank-owned company, that's not allowed. But who the hell am I to say from 1,500 miles away, what's best for Steve's customers in Woodbury, Minnesota?

Of course, some people need structure. Some people must have somebody telling them to come in at 8:00 AM and leave for lunch at 12:00 PM and then come back at 1:00 PM and leave at 5:00 PM. They need an authority figure telling them not to answer their phone on Saturday and Sunday. These kinds of people usually don't fit very well with us because they can't structure their own life. They can't lead. Somebody else has to lead for them.

Remember how I had said earlier, in 1994 that I was introduced to the mortgage business because I had a sh*tty loan officer, and a sh*tty processor when I was financing my first house? The processor said, "If you think you can do it better, do it yourself."

I started taking courses immediately. I wanted to lead myself.

Section II

Mind Your Business

Chapter 8: The Most Important Business Lessons You'll Ever Learn:

Part I

"Business wise, I have always learned valuable lessons, so I don't regret any decisions I have made." ~Kiana Tom

Now, that I've shared where I've come from and how I've gotten here, I want to leave you with some tips that will help you shortcut your success in your business.

Number one: you must have a can-do attitude in business. It doesn't matter what technology you have or don't have. If you don't have a can-do attitude, then nothing is going to work for you. You cannot find a silver bullet out there to make business happen. You have to make it happen. Your attitude will help you make your business happen.

Number two: I see a lot of people ask this question: "What's the best CRM to use?" Let me shoot straight with you: That's about one of the dumbest questions I've ever seen or heard in my life. The best CRM is the one that you will actually use. Some of them have better bells and whistles. Some of them have flashier features or cooler email campaigns, but by the time you get done looking for whatever it is that you're looking for, all of a sudden, a new and "improved" one hits the market. You simply need to make the commitment to yourself. If you get a CRM, use the CRM to its full potential. Period. While you're using that CRM, it's still perfectly acceptable to find a piece of technology that will be more aligned with your business.

If you have poor technology and products, it can hold you back. Think of it this way. You wouldn't want to ask your local banker for a half-million-dollar loan while wearing flip-flops, cutoff shorts, and a muscle shirt. Why? Because you're not necessarily dressing for success. This is a small deviation to what we talked about earlier, wearing what you want to work. Your choices need to be relevant and acceptable for what you are trying to accomplish in your business. So, you probably want to be on time. You probably want to be well-dressed. You probably want to be clean, and you probably want to be as well-spoken as possible as opposed to using slang. Making these choices gives you a better shot in what you are trying to accomplish.

Number three: starting a business requires that you also come up with some sort of a marketing plan. But where do you start when everything is overwhelming, and you don't know the priorities? When I hear this question, I think it is absolutely wonderful, and beautiful. Let's consider what has always worked no matter what year we happen to be in. I'm talking about what we call belly to belly, or face to face marketing. I'm referencing the good, old-fashioned, handshake in the public eye. Social media has killed personal interaction. It's a shame, but if more people got out and actually had coffee together or made appointments if more people showed up and allowed themselves to be seen, they and you would be in a much better place than any of your competition sitting behind a keyboard, stroking out.

To start, find a product or service that you like and that you can explain well. If you're new to the business, figure out what sounds interesting, by doing some research about the topic, and I mean dive into it. Spend eight hours a day and find what it is that you like. Become an expert. Let's say you started in the mortgage business; one of the products you might check out is a rehab loan or what would be called a

203k or a 203ks loan. You may never ever work with these loans, but if you educate yourself into becoming the known expert on a specific product, then it's pretty apparent you also know other products.

When you tell me, you are the best in the mortgage business at X, and that I can trust you with whatever ancillary product questions I have on a mortgage loan, I know you've already put in the time to learn about one specialty. So, it makes sense in my mind that you would be able to relate to other products. This concept goes for nearly anything. Real estate agents can up their game. They can shift to higher-priced sales, and higher-priced listings if they make themselves an expert in a specific area catering to this clientele.

This next topic works well with your plan to expand what you are offering. If you up your productivity by changing your client list, it stands to reason your team should be able to keep up. Training your team is probably the most valuable part of having an office with other individuals. If you expect people to do what it is that you want without telling them, then you will always fail. They will always fail because they don't know the expectations that you put in front of them. Make training your team a priority that will be addressed continuously. You will especially need to spend time here as you grow and your positions or job titles change; hell, as people change. Make it a point to regularly bring your team up to date on what it is you expect of them.

Now, there are times when this plan will fail you. Sometimes, people just do not have the aptitude to do the job that you've assigned them. It's like the joke I always make. I could probably process the hell out of one loan a month because I am not detail oriented but give me more, and it is less challenging and easier for me to work. But if I am charged with explaining a product I'm interested in learning about it, it's much different. I appreciate doing it, and so it is easier and more enjoyable for me. The work seems effortless. Remember to inspect what you expect. Train people on how you want tasks done. When you do that, they will never fail, and you will never fail because you'll both be continuously growing.

Train people that you're bringing up to train others. There's only one of you, and most likely, if you're a business owner, your highest and best use of your time is creating revenue. Your job is to close business and make deals happen, so it's probably not in your best interest, and it's probably not your best use of time to train somebody to do detailed work. You can find a person on your team who will likely be better at conducting this type of training than you. So, train up so you can create trainers you can use on your team.

When you decide how you will delegate and who will train, keep in mind what brings in the greatest amount of revenue for your efforts. What it is that you could do to train somebody to do part of your task for you? I'll give you a prime example. Years ago, I used to cut my own grass. I enjoyed doing it because it took my mind off everything else. The problem was, I would spend eight to 10 hours cutting my grass. I would mow it one direction, be dissatisfied with the way it looked, and then I would mow it in a different direction. It still wouldn't be good enough, so I would run out and buy a new lawnmower blade. Guess what? When I didn't like that lawnmower blade, I would buy a new lawnmower.

Then because I'd bought a new lawnmower, I had to start all over again. I would follow the same crazy cycle with my trimmer, and edger, while I was pruning any of my bushes, or even mulching. It didn't matter what I was working on in the yard, I obsessed, and this was not a good use of my time. What I learned was if I paid somebody to do that job for me and I drove home in the evening, and it was all done, I didn't pay attention to the details as much as I did when I'd done it myself, and it looked absolutely wonderful! I was simply letting somebody else who knew that job better than me do that job, so it wasn't such a waste of my time.

Delegating the lawn work had another benefit. I could identify the mandatory processes I needed because I wasn't wasting time on what was better left with someone else.

You also need to define your mandatory processes.

But before you even get started, you better have your "go get it" attitude ready. You will need to get up every day no matter what and go get what is yours. You've got to gain business. You've got to gain relationships. You have to plan what it is that you're going to do today, tomorrow, next week, next month, six months from now, and even next year to know how your business is going to look as time goes by. You have to continue to plan on what you want to happen.

If you are only looking at tomorrow, you have no idea what six months will bring. You have no idea what one year is going to bring, and you no idea how to rotate or pivot when a dramatic event happens in your business, or in your industry. You need to continue to improve your processes, continue to improve your systems and always look at the future.

A lot of people talk about plan B, and truthfully, I'm not a fan of plan B. If you're making a plan B, I think it implies that you're planning to fail on your plan A. As long as you do your plan A and you're nimble enough to move with market changes or if anything happens in your business, then by paying attention to plan A and sticking to plan A, your mind isn't distracted and going elsewhere.

Stay true to what you need to focus on for your business. Some people regard their businesses with a broader vision, and so they waste time in areas that don't need attending to (yet).

People waste their money on investing, and it absolutely drives me nuts when salespeople try and sell to people in businesses. In the mortgage business, I have heard people specifically say, "If you close one more loan off of this, it pays for itself. If everybody closed one more loan off of one more thing they were sold, they would have so much business; they wouldn't have time for anything else."

Avoid investing your money or time on what isn't a business asset. Buying one more piece of software probably will not do anything for you. Buying one more class, one more anything you don't need and that will take your eye off the ball is probably not a good idea. Why don't you master what you have already, and then as you continue to grow, do the research for what it is you're trying to grow toward, and what you're trying to accomplish as opposed to listening to a salesperson sell you something? A more conservative effort will pay off.

When discussing the fundamentals of business, it is vital that you put maintaining your integrity on the list. Why is it never worth it to compromise your integrity? Integrity and morals should be the number one target in any business. If you know something is not right, and I think that we all learned at about the age of four what right and wrong are, then there is no excuse for choosing to do wrong. This is inherent in human beings in my opinion. You are going to screw up in your business but using excuses to explain why a person made an unethical choice or even why someone broke the law is inexcusable.

Our parents have instilled in us what is right and wrong. Every time I've ever done anything wrong, I knew it was wrong, and I knew what the consequences were, or that there would be consequences. If I had a curfew of 10:00, it was not a good idea to call my parents at 10:30 to say I was going to be late. By that time, I already knew that I was going to be late.

People don't realize when you do the wrong thing others see it, and they will also see if you're willing to compromise your integrity, ethics or morals. If you're willing to compromise your morals, ethics or integrity on say, pinning the blame on someone else in the office, then others will see you as your true self. They will know who you really are, and what it is you're willing to do to gain what you want.

Now, let's segue into pinpointing the signs of people who you don't want to work with. This has always been a tough factor for me. Most of the time, you can tell when you're not going to be a fit with somebody. It's complicated for me sometimes, because I am a trusting soul. I trust people to a fault, and I make a joke about it because my wife trusts no one, and I trust almost everyone. Throughout my life of hiring people and working with them, I've learned to spot who I can trust very quickly. Whether or not I act or react upon it is something that I have to practice and improve for myself.

For example, I've brought people on who have told me that they're producers and then they have shown the exact opposite. I've made the mistake of giving people way too much rope to hang themselves, and in the process of hanging themselves, they also hung me. These instances have cost me a tremendous amount of time, and money. If

I could give one piece of advice to anyone, it would be, to begin with, your gut feeling. When you figure out that your new hire or new decision you've made is wrong, you need to cut those ties or remedy the situation as soon as possible because it will not get any better. You will not gain that money back. You will not gain that time back, and you will not gain back that compromise you made with yourself or them.

There's an old saying that I agree with in part: "Be slow to hire, quick to fire." I don't know how much I agree with the slow to hire part; I completely agree with being quick to fire. You know that it's wrong. You know that these people are not a good fit. Get rid of them as soon as possible because they're a cancer to you and to the people around them. If you don't, their peers will see that you are willing to put up with someone who is not a team player. When they observe this, then they will start questioning your morals, ethics, and your integrity as well. In other words, they will question you.

You can ask yourself a couple of questions to get clear on the truth of the situation: *Is this person as sharp as I think?*

Are they as smart as they're supposed to be? Are they as good as I think they should be to run a business? It's important to know the answers to these questions. As time goes on, the need to know these questions will get more intense, and they will rise to the surface.

What happens when people take the low road? There is a point where you always have to protect yourself, protect your business, and most of all, protect your coworkers. Sometimes, you do have to get down to someone's level. I know that that sounds cliché. It goes against what people have told you. But when some people don't understand and cannot grasp and respect the best decision, sometimes, you do have to stoop. I'm not saying go to the bottom as fast as you can. I'm not saying that you should ever compromise your morals, ethics, or integrity. The reason I stress this is simply because sometimes people can only understand why they shouldn't do something when you explain it to them in words and consequences they can understand. If they make a crappy decision and it doesn't work out for them, they get it. They get the drama and the way that life always seems to be against them. So, you may need to communicate with them in a different manner than you normally would.

Go back, to when you think your integrity has been compromised. It's very hard for humans to admit they're wrong. The guilt will eat you up. I am a fan of failure. I know that sounds completely asinine, but the more that you fail, the smarter, better, and the more nimble and agile you are in life. If you've ever been in a situation where you've compromised your integrity, the best thing to do is admit it to yourself. Then reason with yourself and come up with a response and an answer to let others know.

When you hide these things, you're only trying to hide them from yourself, which you cannot do. And you cannot hide what you have done from others because they have seen and know about it. Hiding it will not only eat you up; it makes other people think differently of you. One of the best things I've ever been told came from one of my friends and co-workers, Patrick Queally. He told me years ago when I hired him to come on as a branch manager that he had done more research on me than anybody else he'd ever talked to. On the subject of integrity, he said he has two different thoughts: "Either I am who I say I am, and I'm the most honest, moral, and integrity-driven person, or I know where all the bodies are hidden, and people are afraid, to tell the truth." He told me: "I'm going to take the first one."

You might think once you have all your business ducks in a row that you will also be bestowed with the most perfect clients. But cuing into your ideal client takes work and thought. So, you might even encounter a circumstance where you have to fire a client, and maybe you will even do it because they demonstrated a lack of integrity. This might surprise you, but depending on the situation, you will want to fire the client as fast as you possibly can. One, you never want to work with somebody who doesn't have any scruples. You also don't want to work with somebody who is a time waster and a money waster. For example, if you're a real estate agent, don't put somebody in your car, and don't meet them if they haven't been vetted to find out if they even qualify for a loan. Don't show multiple houses to a prospect who's doing nothing but wasting your time, and truly just collecting decorating tips.

How many hours did you spend with that one client who was a time waster of yours? How many clients who needed your help did you actually pass up because of that one client? If you have a personality conflict, I can also see that as a reason not to work with someone.

Most likely, neither one of you will be happy at the end, and your main goal is to get referral customers from every one of your clients, so if you're not going to make this person happy, you will not get anything back in return. There's an old saying: "If you make somebody happy, they may tell one person. If you make a person upset, they'll tell 10." Remember that as you're taking on your new clients. Never forget your ethics as you are dealing in business.

We might all know of CEOs who probably should not be the face or the voice of the company because of the mistakes they've frequently made. Look at some of the companies in existence today, and you'll see what their stock prices and stock values do on a daily basis. These numbers will show you who may or may not be the right person to run or own a company. This supports exactly what I said before: No matter the way you conduct yourself; people will find out. The value of your business will reflect your behavior.

It's possible to run a company morally and ethically where revenue and money do not have the main presence in the decisions that are made day to day. So, a company that pulls in more money may not necessarily be at risk of falling into an ethical pitfall. High revenue or low revenue, whoever is at the wheel is in charge of how the company will behave, and how other people view that company.

No CEO answers to themselves. They answer to a board. They answer to a customer. They answer to a market. That's something very important that I think people forget as they're growing their business. As you grow a majority of the most impactful business decisions and the direction your company chooses to go will be in the hands of other people besides yourself.

We come across moral and ethical challenges on a daily basis. It's what we decide to do and what the people around us see that will make the difference in our lives and in our company.

Chapter 9: The Most Important Business Lessons You'll Ever Learn:
Part II

"Man's mind, once stretched by a new idea, never regains its original dimensions." ~Oliver Wendell Holmes

We forget: employers have a responsibility. It's irresponsible watching businesses lay people off continuously. It's irresponsible when people have too much overhead and don't watch the market to see what's going on. Although I can see the reasons why, I don't necessarily like it, and I don't use it in my business philosophy. As you watch some of these big box banks laying off hundreds of people as we go into a slower market, it shows greed. That company didn't care about those people when they hired them. They want you to think that they care about them as they lay them off, but that's not true. All they've done was create more problems for their former employee by giving them a false sense of security for a time when they had no intention of keeping them on.

I know taking this position will get me some boos and frowns and negative comments, and I don't give a f*ck. I mean it. You have a responsibility as an employer. Just like an employee has a responsibility to you, you have a responsibility to control what you can control. If you can't see the future and try to abide by it, and if you just hire people for them to have a job, you're not being responsible. Not to your company, or yourself and not to the people you employ.

When you are just starting out, it can be difficult to understand the 30,000-foot view. But as a seasoned professional, I can see that some of the turns these businesses have taken could have been prevented.

Don't tap into the "if you build it, they will come" mentality and expect to see success. There has to be an interest in what you are offering; there has to be a market. There has to be somebody else marketing it. I see a tremendous amount of small businesses that I absolutely fall in love with. They use social media to market. They use SEO, they use websites, and they use word of mouth to get that information out. Because of this, they do really, really well.

I don't like the use of false information to grow a business. I don't like employing scare tactics to get sales rolling. If I were starting a new business, out of the clear blue sky, one, I would make sure there was a market for it. Two, I would make sure that I market it better than anybody else. Three, I would make sure that the hardest working employee at my business, was me. That I led by example. Because a couple of results will happen. If you're the hardest working employee at your business, people will see that, and they will either flock to it, or they will flock away from it. Regardless, it helps you decide who gets to stay and who gets to go.

I've known a tremendous amount of people who were highly educated, but who were so damn lazy they couldn't get out of their own way. I've known people who barely could make it through high school. They were some of the best people I've ever met in my life. These are the kinds of people that you would lie down and take a bullet for in a heartbeat to make sure that your vision comes through and that your vision comes true for everyone around them.

Matter of fact, I've known a lot of people who have gone out and started their own business, and I will help and support them all day long. But for those who don't want to, I try and supply a great home and place for them to be, so they will be proud of where they work, and proud of their coworkers.

This is in contrast to an entirely different type of person: the entrepreneur or businessperson who uses excuses to be unproductive or unprofitable.

Let me use LinkedIn as a prime example. Have you ever noticed if you post on LinkedIn that you got a new job, everybody in the world congratulates you and tells you what a super company you're with and blah, blah, blah? But if you ever post that you started your own business, for some reason two-thirds or more of the people have to be negative about it. They are obsessed with telling you that all of these businesses fail, and the average restaurant only stays open for nine months...so you're going to fail. When I think of this example, it reminds me that we live in such a jacked-up society. The fact is everybody can start their own business, no matter how big it is and no matter how big their goals.

There's a lot of people out there doing their own thing in business. Look at all the social media darlings right now. Go to a dollar store; see what's on the shelves. While you're in that dollar store, go on Amazon and eBay and jot down the retail prices of what people are buying. Buy everything that they have on the shelves; take it home and start your own Amazon store or your own eBay Store. Boom, you have a new business!

What you have created for yourself is called margin, and that's what every business does. You're giving goods to people who actually want them. So, I don't want to hear the excuse that not everybody can start their own business. There is a way and form to do this, and I want to encourage anybody and everybody to start their own business of some kind.

If you're a photographer, there's no reason why you can't take pictures on the side, on the weekends, and after work. The same applies to video crews. If the expense is prohibitive, then save up. If you know the camera's going to cost you $1,000, save $100 a month for the next 10 months, then go buy that camera. Find that camera on Craigslist. Let people know what it is that you're doing.

Once your doors are open, don't discount your prices. It drives me insane when people ask to discount the prices. Because you're actually going to go out of business at some point in time if you discount your prices. You can't offer your service for anything below what you're advertising.

If, for instance, you're charging somebody $200 to take pictures of their house, and somebody else wants to pay you $50 or says, "I will refer you to all of my friends, and you'll end up with so much business, you can't handle it," and you accept this BS offer, then all you're doing is wasting your camera and your time. You're wasting your gas and everything else you have sunk into your business for a hope that's not there. If you do this, people will also think of you in a different light, and it will be other than as a professional. Never once have I gone to my dentist or my doctor to find they've discounted their prices while I was there. At the same time, not once have I ever gone to my dentist or my doctor and asked them to discount their prices. So why would anybody else discount their prices, just for the possibility of gaining new business? Don't discount yourself, because when you discount your prices, you're discounting yourself.

Standing by your prices has everything to do with confidence and having an optimistic mindset. I don't think you can run a business as a pessimist. It will be harder to defend your right to charge what you are worth if you don't believe in yourself and your business.

I do think there are people who are pessimistic, and who have hired somebody else to run or build their business. I don't think that's a good fit, because the person that's the optimist who's selling the service if they don't feel good about the service they're selling or the person they're selling to, it could end quite tragically, and negatively.

You have to be an optimist, even when everybody else is pessimistic. If you start your own business, and somebody is pessimistic about you starting that kind of business, or a business in general, don't listen to those people. Listen to customers. Listen to the market. Don't listen to pessimism. Believe in yourself and your abilities and align yourself with people who feel the same way.

I don't put up with gossip. I don't put up with BS, and I don't put up with people who are cancers inside my own shop. If somebody's walking around talking about how horrible something is, or how f*cked up something is, get rid of them today. Your business cannot handle it. Because what you'll find out is, these people can ruin really good people, just by having their ear a little bit.

If you're a naturally negative person, here's what you can do. Stop. Find somebody you can relate to. Whether it be Tony Robbins or Gary V., whoever it may be that will help you get rid of this mindset. But there is no room in this world for people who are negative. Stay away from them. Keep your business away from them. Keep anybody and everybody you know away from them. People don't know this little social media tip. If you have people who are negative in your life, who write negative posts or share negative pictures or negative comments, it carries over to your page, to your site, and everything else. People are turned off by these messages, and they will not follow you. They will actually unfriend you.

But, subconsciously they will also wonder what's wrong with you. They will wonder why you allow such content. So, if this human being in your circle is talking negatively all the time, what is it about you that likes that, or tolerates that? When people are negative it doesn't only affect them; it affects everyone around them, including their friends, co-workers, their boss, and employees. This is something that you have to get rid of. I'm telling you now if you have somebody like this in your life, you need to fire them from your life and business immediately. Today. Because it does not get any better.

These are just lessons, and everything in life is just an education.

This is actually one of my favorite sayings, and it is a way that I approach business. Every day, we are learning. You know the old saying, "If you're the smartest guy in the room, you're in the wrong room." It's quite funny how you can learn things about your business from other businesses.

This past weekend we were at a hotel where I happen to be a diamond member. At this moment in time, in October of 2018, I have over two million points with this particular hotel. The hotel had 28 rooms and two elevators, but one of them is broken down continuously; in fact, it was out of order the whole time we were there. We happen to live in Houston, Texas where there are multiple elevator companies, and if this had been a problem in Houston, it would have been fixed. But it wasn't, and so it was causing problems for everyone who was staying there for work. They had to wait 20 minutes for an elevator to get them from their floor down to the bottom floor, so that they could go to work. I even heard a story as I was standing at the front desk. One guy shared that he had actually been late for work because he had to wait 20 minutes for the elevator.

To top it off, the front desk help all had attitude problems, and they talked down to almost everybody over and over again. I heard this when I was right there at the desk with everyone else. Now, the one good part of this situation is that by having over two million points with this particular company, I get to put my experience into a survey and let it be known how bad this hotel is. One thing that two million points will get you is a lot of experience. So, I've been to a lot of this brand's hotels all over this country and all over this world.

I'm hoping that they will pay attention to my feedback. But, it also lets me know what's acceptable and what's not acceptable. What this particular hotel chain is doing (or not doing) is not acceptable. Every other hotel I've stayed at with the millions of points I have is respectful at the front desk. They're on top of problems. If they're remodeling, they apologize, and there are signs up everywhere letting you know how much they appreciate you for being there. They tell you at every opportunity how much they appreciate you for being a diamond member. But this one particular franchise did a really poor job with their customer service, and it will affect their business when I need to rent another 30 or 40 rooms next year for the same exact summit. I won't be using theirs.

The cost of the rooms was probably $150 a night or more, so that's $5,000 a day, for four days that they're going to miss out on. This is on top of all the bar tabs and other ancillary costs my guys racked up during their stay.

Their mindset in how they were handling customer service has a direct effect on the owner's pocketbook.

This is a good lead into discussing what it means to have a success mindset because obviously, that hotel did not have it and they did not teach their staff that either.

When people are successful, two kinds of people gravitate to them. You have the people who admire them and think that they're absolutely wonderful and great, which they are in whatever aspect it is that they participate, whether it be baseball, politics, business, or anything else. Then you've got a small subsection of people who hate others for being successful. Look at the professional athletes, and you'll see there's always somebody who loves them, and there's always somebody who hates them for some strange, stupid reason.

There are also always comparisons. The same concept applies to politics and business. When someone's successful, the greater majority admire them, while a smaller subsection of people just wants to be jackasses, and either be heard, or they might be intent on casting their doubt on the picture for some strange reason.

Having a successful mindset, and having success as your goal every day, is imperative to adopt every day. This is not a choice; it's actually a decision. You make the decision every single day that this is what you're going to do.

One of the things I tell my guys is, "I love failure." I actually promote failure. Because the person who doesn't fail never does anything. It's actually music to my ears when my guys try really hard to put something together, and it doesn't necessarily work the first time. Or it's one or two degrees off. The look on their face or the sound in their voice, or the tone in the email when it comes across when they have succeeded with those one or two little tweaks, puts a smile on my face and a smile in my heart.

See, the more that you fail, the more that you will succeed. If you've never failed, you've never done a damn thing. You've sat on the sidelines and been a Monday morning quarterback and never done anything to help promote this world, this company, or this country. So, if you're reading this and this section of the book turns you off, please give it to somebody who it will help. Because I don't know if it will help you.

If you need a jump on what to do to change your mindset and to make traction, here are some ideas.

Reading is one of the best activities. Read from people who are actually excited about life, who are happy to be in business, who are happy to be part of a society that promotes this type of mindset.

Remember, we're in the greatest country in the world. Every day it gets better and better. You have the ability and choice to make it better or worse. If you make it worse, you're tearing down your own life, but you are also negatively impacting other people's lives. If you have family, you're destroying part of your family. If you have co-workers, you're making yourself look worse. If this is you, you have to remove this mindset from your life.

This is the biggest takeaway from this book that your mindset will control your success.

Barry Habib's Book Endorsement and Business Bonus

Leadership

Leadership's a very big responsibility. The role of the leader is to bring out the best in people, and that's a lot easier said than it is to do. When you're trying to inspire others, it's important to understand that you should never have someone do or instruct someone else to do a task or take an action mechanically. You need to give them the reasoning or the "why" behind it. So many times, companies and leaders put out a policy without seeking buy-in. I'm not saying that you need to take a consensus, but you need to articulate that life is about choices.

There is no perfect. Every single thing that you do will have some good aspects and some bad. If someone were ill and they went to the physician, and the physician knew that a medication could cause a rash, nausea, convulsions, and other side effects, the warnings would scare the heck out of the patient. Why would they ever take that drug? This is an example of life not being about perfect but being about choices. Ultimately, it's better to take the medication even though there are side effects than it is to remain sick.

The cure is better than the side effects.

As leaders, we should not simply put out what the policy is because everybody will point to the side effects; a great leader articulates the journey, all of it. A great leader will let people in on the full truth. We're intelligent enough to have explored the different options, and we need to share that we as leaders have done so. Of course, one option is doing nothing. But if you do that, you also run the risk that this is the worst option for you and your business.

While the doctor deliberates over what to prescribe, because of the side effects that could be experienced, the patient could become much more ill.

Communication is key. Communication is taking a thought, from your brain, and positioning it in the person's brain or in the brains of the group of people with whom you are trying to communicate.

The point is: the thought that's in your brain went on a journey before you formulated it. The mistake that so many people make and the reason why we have such bad communication is because the speaker formulates that thought and then decides they are going to implant the result into somebody else's brain. After that, they wonder why they and the recipient aren't on the same page.

What you need to do with your team instead is to metaphorically, hold their hand and take them through that journey and how you arrived at your destination. Then when you share the mental path you have been on, when you implant the end result, you have a much higher degree of probability that that person will, at least, be able to understand what you have shared. They will be able to evaluate it. They might not agree with it, but when you take this approach, you have a much greater chance of them understanding it.

Inspiration is vital for our teammates. If you instill this in a rah-rah fashion, that's ephemeral, or short lasting. If you want that inspiration to be enduring and meaningful, then you have to really touch that person and get them to believe in what you're doing. Usually, leaders put out the mission statement, and it sounds good on paper, but then they go about their business and completely forget about that statement and the reason why they are in business. People will believe in you as a leader and be inspired by you when you allow them to see how you handle your business in the face of adversity.

It's a lot easier to be a great leader when everything's going right, but a truly exceptional leader is one who can show character in the face of adversity.

Relationships

Your team needs to know how you consider the customer and your relationships. If you can make that individual, who you are leading, proud to say, "Wow, I aspire to those ethics. I aspire to those principals; they are always concerned with the customer's best interests," that's how you start to inspire people. When they believe in what they're doing, when they believe in the product, when they believe in the company, when they believe in the philosophy, that's much more critical than if they were to merely believe in a mission statement. Mission statements are important, yes, but the actions behind the statement are more important.

This also holds true when we look at the dynamic relationship between real estate agents and mortgage professionals.

Relationships with real estate agents are tricky to handle and to keep perspective on because there's a lot of emotion involved. To some degree, the mortgage professional is controlling the Realtor's livelihood, because if the Realtor is entrusting you with a transaction, they expect to see that transaction executed. If that transaction doesn't close the real estate agent will receive less than they expected after having done quite a bit of work. So, many times, a Realtor's judgment can get clouded, and reasoning can go out the window because the Realtor wants to know how you are going to get the transaction to close. They don't care how you finish the job, and they certainly won't care why a job wasn't completed when you had promised it would be. They are less sympathetic to the obstacles that you have as a mortgage professional and the difficulties that you have with a client who promised you one thing and delivered something else.

What can you do to become a better mortgage originator?

You need to become better at being the bearer of bad news, whether it is delivered to the Realtor or the customer.

The ability to have those difficult conversations will serve you well.

Making Mistakes

Don't be afraid of making mistakes.

It's when things don't work out that we learn. I discovered this early on in my life. When I was a kid, I had too much energy, after college, to take an office job. So, I sold stereo equipment out of the trunk of my car. I recruited all my friends to work with me and turned it into a successful business. Then I started buying real estate with the profits I made.

I grew up extremely poor. My dad passed away when I was a young boy. My mom worked in a sweatshop sewing dresses. When I started selling stereo equipment, one of the lessons I learned was that when things go wrong, it can be a great opportunity. Since I was selling electronic equipment, there were times when things didn't work correctly. The customer, who had purchased this equipment from a young kid, selling it out of his trunk, likely felt that they would never see me again. But they were very pleasantly surprised when they would call and have me respond by coming out and exchanging the equipment. In fact, they were so pleased, that they quite often felt obligated to purchase even more equipment from me or to recommend me to someone else.

The big life lesson for me was that problems could become huge opportunities if handled correctly.

Righting the wrong is your chance to rise above, to do the right thing, and to build trust with that customer. Sales is all about trust. So many people have a problem being the bearer of bad news. But that's what builds trust. When you go to a restaurant and order an item off the menu from the server, and the server looks at you and says, "Don't get that. It's been sitting." They're giving you bad news, but you will trust them more in that instant. You'll probably give them a bigger tip and likely ask for them again.

It's amazing that today, it's very difficult to get people to pick up the phone. Texting has overtaken talking, and I feel bad for those individuals who have lost the art of conversation because they'd rather text. Yes, texting is simpler, but there's no replacement for the voice inflection, emotion and the understanding that comes through when you talk to someone.

You will learn so much from interactions with other people.

Trust

When we look at the relationship between the salesperson and the customer in every transaction, metaphorically or in real life, they're usually on opposite sides of the table from each other. We have to change that narrative. Get on the same side of the table with your arm around their shoulder.

Walk through what they need to do. Stop selling and start advising.

Think of your customer as a family member, who is going to be entering into an important real estate transaction, which you are unable to handle personally. They called you up and said, "What should I watch out for?" Give them advice in that manner... You wouldn't be selling them; you would be advising them as to which questions they should ask. So, when you talk to your customer, it's okay to present your product, positively and highlight the features, but you should also show your customer the pitfalls.

This is how you quickly and effectively build trust.

Most people are afraid to do that because they're afraid they might lose their commission. But the risk of losing your commission is dwarfed by gaining trust because trust endures. Trust is what gets you that repeat customer, and trust is what allows you to maintain price integrity and to get referrals from them. This is the essence of being an advisor and not being afraid. Don't make that customer feel like they've got a bullseye on their back with your commission as a target.

What's good for them, is much more important than if you get paid. If they're going to do the transaction, they're going to do the transaction.

Somebody's going to get a commission on it. It might as well be you if you're giving them the right advice.

Gratitude

I learned from that period in my life that we could complain that it could be better, but no matter where you are, it could always be a lot worse. As bad as you think it is, it can get downright tragic. You have to be thankful for your life and business.

I start off every day with gratitude and prayer. It's important. In the morning begin with being thankful for all of the great things you have in your life. When you do that it's astounding to see how your perspective shifts.

When I was younger, and we were so poor, I remember riding in the subway with my mom and seeing people in worse shape.

My mom had this little gold-colored purse. I remember the noise it made when she'd unsnap it, reach in, and take some coins out. I recall riding the subway with her, and when she would see someone else in need, she wanted to help them. We had nothing, but she would give the little she had to other people. When she did that, she would look at me and say, "It's good to help people." While you do it for that person who needs it, in the moment, you really do it for you.

When someone says, "Thank you" when I do something for them, I turn right back around and say, "No, no, thank you. Thank you for allowing me to experience this good feeling that I have about myself. Thank you for letting me do that."

The Current State of Affairs

When you are in a position with that customer where trust is established, then if it's a good fit, you've got a customer already. The hardest part is not getting more sales from the same customer. It's getting the first sale. If you've done it right and if it's correct for the customer, you can deepen the relationship with them. It's a lot easier to ask for their continued patronage when trust has already been established.

People who have been in the business for even 10 years have not been in a natural mortgage or real estate market environment. It's been artificially subsidized by the Fed. Even by the European Central Bank (ECB) because all the bond markets are interrelated and connected. Interest rates have been artificially held down. Volatility levels have been muted, because of the Fed buying, but recently, when the Fed and the ECB stopped buying, we embarked on a new paradigm, a more natural market, one that you would have to go back 10 years or longer to relate to. We've already started to see a dramatic increase in volatility, which will continue.

This makes it more important than ever to be educated on the financial markets as you navigate clients through these volatile times.

Why You Need to Become an Advisor

Even if you've been in the business 20 years, you start to develop habits from the climate of the last 10 years. We've gotten a little bit spoiled, but we're about to enter a different environment. That's why being an advisor is so important. But it doesn't mean you slap the word on your name tag, and now you're an advisor.

A professional boxer trains a thousand minutes for every minute in the ring. Ask yourself how many minutes you are training before you get on the phone. Is it zero? Well, that's why you're not converting. Are you really putting in the work?

I love sales because sales is fair. For the most part, you will get out what you put in. As much as I love athletics, it isn't very fair. Regardless of how much effort you put in, you may not have enough God-given ability to become professional. In high school, I was a good athlete. Then I went to college, and it seemed like a lot of the other kids got far better than I did. I wasn't bad, and I sure worked hard. Man, I was the first to practice. I was the last one to leave. I practiced at home. I was into it, but you know what? I just didn't have the gifts. Others who were faster and jumped higher had more natural ability than I did. No matter how much I tried, it wasn't going to happen. That's not true in sales. In sales, it doesn't matter if your competitor is faster than you. It doesn't matter if they're stronger. It doesn't matter if they can jump higher than you. You only need one thing, and that's heart. You can win if you have the heart.

Are you willing to put in the work? Are you willing to dedicate yourself to gaining the knowledge it takes to be an advisor? Are you willing to make a difference for that customer because you've attained the coaching or the tools, the resources, and the education to, literally, change that customer's life for the better? Then you'll win. But so few people are willing to do that, and that's the beauty of sales. It is fair. You're going to get out what you put in. But you have to put in the right stuff.

Some people say, "I've been in the business 10 years." The question I have is, "Is it 10 years or is it one year 10 times?" There's a very big difference between the two. That education is critical in understanding how you can benefit the customer. These are really important insights for the loan originator today, because, as I said, the market is very different than it has been in the past.

Technology is moving so rapidly that originators are under attack. Technology is trying desperately to replace them, and they better pay attention.

Remember when there were travel agents everywhere? Younger folks might say, "What's a travel agent? You mean the app on my phone?" No, there were actually people in those positions who were made extinct when they were replaced by technology. Why? Because they were not advisors. They were salespeople or information gatherers.

You would think that the epitome of a non-commoditized transaction, would be taking a vacation because you work all year and then have a precious two weeks to yourself. During those two weeks, don't you want the restaurants to be right? Don't you want the hotel space to be right? Don't you want the resort to be what you want? The surroundings, the excursions, the sights, don't you want it to be meaningful? Think about all you've sacrificed...waking up early for work, working late, enduring aggravation. Now you've finally got these two weeks of vacation. Do you really want to make that a commodity and leave it to chance, and then have to wait another whole year in case it wasn't perfect? This is where a travel agent needed to shine because it's about the experience. But somewhere along the line, the travel agent became a commodity.

Think about a mortgage. Think about a real estate transaction. These are not commodities. If I asked you what two homes were exactly alike, the answer would be none, because they each sit on their own piece of land. They're each going to have their own view. It is impossible for these homes to be a commodity because they have to be different. While two mortgages might have the same loan amount, interest rate, and payment, the way it individually impacts the borrower is totally different because each borrower has unique needs and will feel the effects of that transaction differently. While the interest rate or payment might be the same, the way it affects each customer is unique.

To view either of these transactions as a commodity is foolish. That is a false narrative people believe. It's the fault of the originator who doesn't change the narrative by building the education to communicate that this is an experience. Individuals need to be shown how the management of their experience, and their choice of product can greatly impact them.

In an environment where interest rates were lower a few years ago, and the current rate is higher, you have challenges. It's a lot easier when interest rates are declining because you have the opportunities for refinancing. You've got opportunities to purchase a larger home with cheaper financing options.

The reality today is that consumers are not even thinking about refinancing because they have been able to obtain a much lower rate over the past few years. In fact, it's almost worn as a badge of honor, which allows them to brag to their friends about grabbing the lowest rates possible. This thought process also exists amongst the mortgage professionals who mistakenly and short-sidedly dismisses even contacting the client about refinancing because they can't wrap their mind around taking the client from a lower interest rate on their existing loan to a higher interest rate refinance. But a true advisor could see that there may be other ways to dramatically help that client through debt consolidation. Most of their past clients have had car loans and credit card debt, which can be rolled into a refinance even at a higher rate, that would radically lower their monthly payment and even allow for their customer to pull out some cash. Taking this a step further, a mortgage advisor can then tell the customer to utilize the monthly payment savings toward paying down the new mortgage, which could, in many cases, cut the term of that loan in half. Imagine saving your client 15 years of mortgage payments, while keeping their overall payment the same as it is now, and at the same time giving them a lump sum of cash to utilize. This is all done by intelligently managing their debts even though you are taking them from a lower existing rate to a higher current rate.

It's far more expensive to have the lowest rate on the wrong strategy than it is to have a competitive rate on the right financial plan for your future.

The same philosophy is true on a move-up purchase, where the existing home has a lower mortgage at a lower rate than the new home the customer is looking to purchase. The payment shock, although within the customer's ability to qualify and repay, gives them pause in moving forward to realize the home of their dreams. The above-mentioned debt consolidation strategy will not only bridge or significantly reduce the payment gap, but it will also allow them a way to pay the new mortgage off sooner and utilize the newly gained equity toward their retirement or their children's college needs.

The other big mistake that mortgage professionals make is that they don't keep in touch with their customers on a regular basis. Many loan originators think they do because of a slick drip campaign they bought which sends the customer a greeting card, but nothing can replace an actual phone call. We've all heard of economic cycles, but your clients have both life and credit cycles. Their need for money, whether it's a lump sum or cash flow, will change dramatically over time. This is based on their life cycles— whether it's a job change, change in marital status, the birth or passing of someone—or any of a multitude of changes that life throws at us. Your client's financial needs will vary throughout time. Think about your personal situation. Haven't things changed over the past few years for you? Having that discussion with them can uncover ways you can better serve them and even if you can't, building that strong relationship and becoming more top-of-mind to your customer will certainly lead to more referrals.

An annual review conversation with your customer will help you continuously add value to that client by addressing their current financial needs.

When we put it all together, by understanding our client's needs as well as understanding the economic landscape, we truly begin to fill the role of an advisor. Having an expertise as well as the ability to articulate the opportunity that real estate presents in your client's market, will set you far above any competitor and make you highly desirable to realtor referral sources. An example of this would be a mortgage advisor's ability to see that the financial landscape suggests there will be a high probability of recession over the next few years. Because they are educated in this area, they know that history tells us that interest rates almost always decline in a meaningful way during recessions, while real estate values tend to hold up well. This will help the mortgage advisor correctly guide their clients in a way that doesn't just look at the mortgage they're doing today, but more importantly, how this mortgage relates to the next mortgage that they will be doing in the future. So, if they see a refinance opportunity on the horizon, it's likely better to take a higher interest rate today that includes as many fees as possible than a lower interest rate with more upfront fees that will never be recuperated because that loan will be refinanced in short order.

In a mortgage professional's effort to please their referral sources and clients, I often hear them say to those referral sources and clients "I am always available." It sure sounds nice, but in reality, no one can always be available.

It's far more important to be an advisor because instead of saying that you're always available, your referral sources and clients will know that you are always worth waiting for.

My Friend Jonny

I was excited to get an opportunity to contribute to this great book. I've been a fan of Jonathan Fowler for a long time. Of course, as a business person, I love his energy. I love his knowledge, and his intelligence, but I also love the fact that Jonny cares. If you get to know him, you will see that very, very quickly, because while again, he is all of those important traits that make him very special, to me, the fact that he cares sincerely and deeply is what makes Jonny a person you feel blessed to call your friend.

He is someone who always has your back, someone you know who will always look out for you ahead of himself. Clients that have used him on the mortgage side are lucky. Individuals who are his teammates and work with him are lucky. People who read this book to get his perspective and understand his passion are very lucky. I know the people who are reading it have those qualities already and what Jonny does is makes it easier for you to express what's in your heart.

Acknowledgments

I want to thank my wife Cassy Fowler for being part of my life for the past 20 years and for being part of this book. I tell people all the time she's my Carmela Soprano. If you ever want to see a woman pissed off, and ready to kill you, try and screw with me and my wife will show you payback.

I want to thank my baby brother for always being there, helping me and being a part of my life. He was one of the greatest gifts I could ever have gotten for that July Christmas.

I want to thank some of my friends throughout the years. Thank you, Gerald Parish. Reid Cashdollar. I want to thank Scott Hogan. I want to thank Chris Moreno. I want to thank the people in my life who actually did something. So, thank you to Sarandos Theocharidis (Sandy).

I want to thank some of the guys, that helped guide me when I was a very young man working in a business that I did not like. Pat Meers, Chuck Warner, Joe Crigler, and Craig

Moorhouse, thank you for being part of my life, and for helping to guide and train me—even when I was a jackass.

I want to thank my father most of all. Wayne Fowler. I absolutely adore and love that man. I miss him every day of my life.

I want to thank my mother, Liza. She's been an inspiration. She made sure that we were taken care of and that we had everything possible that we needed or wanted.

I want to thank my grandfather for loving me and caring for me so much when I was younger. He was my idol. One of the things I joke about is, I know there is no such thing as the afterlife, 'cause if there was, my father and my grandfather, two of the smartest men who have ever walked this earth, would have figured out a way to come back and talk to me.

I want to thank my brother-in-law, my sister-in-law, and my friends and family. Thank you to everyone who has helped me in my life and who have helped to make this book work. It means the world to me.

There are a few teachers in my life that I want to thank, too. One of them was Mr. Mockheart, my fourth-grade teacher. I probably didn't deserve the great treatment I got from him, but he made a huge impact on my life.

I want to thank my high school principal who threw me out of school. This man, who was supposed to be an educator and motivator, actually told me the best I could ever hope for in life was to be a bouncer in a nightclub. The fact that I know that I lead a nicer life, a better life, a happier life, and that I make ten times what he ever made puts a giant grin on my face. I would really like to be able to show that educator how stupid he was for saying what he said to me. I wish I could show him my W-2s. Hopefully, I'm the only one he ever spoke to so horribly.

But I am grateful for that moment in my life as well because that principal's attitude proved to me how strong-willed I actually am. I could have allowed his words to destroy my life, but instead, they only drove me to work my ass off to prove him wrong.

About the Author

Jonathan (Jonny) Fowler has directed national production for the mortgage industry in 50 states and has managed branch office services and national production initiatives. He has been helping retail mortgage branch managers redefine the meaning of success since 1998. Jonny has a knack for bringing the right people to the right opportunity, making it possible for them to not only expand their mortgage businesses but to also grow personally and professionally as they positively impact their communities.

Jonathan manages all national branch recruiting and overall expansion. He works to develop policies and procedures for recruiting, vetting, hiring and retaining top mortgage branch managers. He acts as the company liaison for new branch business planning, opening, and production development.

Made in the USA
Coppell, TX
12 February 2020